the Book of Ghosts

written by
Trent Brandon

The Book of Ghosts

Written by: Trent Brandon
trent@zerotime.com

Cover Art and Artwork: Chris Pugh
Book Design: Chris Pugh, Trent Brandon
Editor: Tiffiny Cope
Publisher Assistant: Tiffiny Cope
Publishing Assistance: BookMasters Inc.

This book is subject to revisions when deemed applicable to keep it current with technical advances in the paranormal field and new scientific research.

Published by,
Zerotime Publishing in Association with Zerotime Paranormal.
Website: http://www.zerotime.com/

ISBN: 0-9703100-7-2
Printed in the United States of America

The Book of Ghosts
Table of Contents

The Book of Ghosts Introduction

Welcome to The Book of Ghosts. Whether this is your first book on the supernatural subject of ghosts or your one hundredth volume, it is the author's hope that you will find this book to be unique and informative. Almost all of the ghost information presented inside the Book of Ghosts is derived directly from years of invaluable Zerotime Paranormal case studies, experiments, and fieldwork. The personal stories graciously provided are the direct result of email correspondence from people around the world to the author through the Zerotime Paranormal website.

The Book of Ghosts was written because the current system used to categorize ghosts is outdated and insufficient to accurately classify the many diverse types of ghosts. It is the purpose of this book to help change a flawed system. The previous system categorized ghosts based on only their actions such as the recurring apparition (a ghost seen over and over in the same location), the deathbed apparition (a ghost of a loved one seen just after their death), and the collective apparition (a ghost seen by many people at the same time), etc. This process works to an extent, but in the end, it falls short of understanding the complicated nature of ghosts. The old process sorts the actions of a ghost, but does not appreciate that these ghostly acts are based on the ghost's personality and experience. The defective system lumps many ghosts into categories based on single actions and leaves out many types of ghosts that do not fit into any of the categories. The system fails to take into account that the individual personality of a ghost defines the ghost.

Ghosts are more than noisy spirits banging on the walls in the night, turning off lights, and locking doors. Ghosts are complex beings trapped in their unique circumstances. To accurately classify ghosts, paranormal researchers have to study and examine the ghost's personalities more than their actions.

The Book of Ghosts provides valuable information on the characteristics, meanings, and personalities of many different types of ghosts. There are numerous new classifications of ghosts listed in this book based on the unique behaviors of each particular ghost, which will help readers and paranormal researchers better understand the mystery behind the ghost. Ghosts cannot be fully understood until there is a realization that ghosts are more character than action. The Book of Ghosts is a passionate examination of the realm of ghosts. Through this book, the hard work of the author and many believers that came before him to advance the scientific and social theories on the enigma of ghosts continues…

The Definition and Characteristics of a Ghost

The technical definition of the word ghost is: "the supernatural manifestation of the disembodied soul or life force of a deceased person or animal," but ghosts are so much more than a simple description. Ghosts are invisible entities of pure energy that can manipulate the natural environment through paranormal methods. A ghost will elude the perceptions of normal reality.

Ghosts are typically thought of as things that go bump in the night. Ghosts are misunderstood and often stereotyped as malicious and dangerous. It has only been in the past few decades that scientists have actually started to study ghosts. Parapsychologists and ghost hunters do their best to determine how and why ghosts exists, but ghosts do very little to help. Ghosts almost always conduct themselves contradictory to what the living has planned. When a parapsychologist needs a ghost to appear, they will never appear, but as soon as the parapsychologist leaves, the ghost will become active.

Ghosts can be male or female. They can appear in any place at anytime. Ghosts can haunt hotels, hospitals, cemeteries, homes, battlefields, churches, abandoned buildings, etc. There is no place that a ghost cannot haunt. Ghosts are most common in places were strange, mysterious or violent and untimely deaths have occurred. Most ghosts do seem to be stuck in one location, but again, there are some categories of ghosts that seem to break the rule and travel.

Ghosts will affect the human senses, but they will affect them in ways that do not seem possible. Ghosts can be heard and felt but not necessarily seen. They can be seen but might not make a sound. They might be standing right in front of a person and yet they cannot be touched. They are on the edge of illusions, but they are real and can influence people and manipulate the natural environment.

Ghosts can appear in lifelike forms looking real and solid just like a living person. Ghosts can also appear in half forms or transparent, in mists, clouds, or orbs. They can also be completely invisible to the human eye. A ghost can be something as small as a single ghostly hand with its finger pointing at a tombstone or something more complicated like a ghost who gets picked up hitchhiking and has a long conversation with the driver just before vanishing from the car without a trace.

Ghosts are capable of manipulating the physical environment by moving, levitating, and breaking objects. They can open and close doors and windows or hide personal items from the living. Ghosts can stack items on top of each other or cause items to fall off of shelves. Ghosts have the ability to interfere with electrical equipment. They can turn lights on and off and can even run electrical appliances that are not plugged in. Ghosts can cause shocks, power surges, or shorts in electrical systems.

There are classes of ghosts that are conscious, intelligent, decision-making manifestations capable of expressing human feelings and emotions and communicating messages. There are also other classes of ghosts that seem oblivious to the world around them and ignore the presence of the living. There are quiet ghosts and ghosts that will bang on the walls for hours without stopping.

Ghosts are a paradox. They are things that should not exist in the normal world. The system of life and death is simple. A person is born, they live out their life, they die, and then their soul moves onto another plane of existence. In the case of a ghost, something is broken in the system. The ghost does not move to another existence.

There is no formula for determining the characteristics of all ghosts. For every theory designed to classify ghosts, there will be a ghost that will break the rules. Ghosts are as unique as snowflakes. Every ghost must be looked at individually to determine what characteristics it will offer. The personality of each ghost must be studied and profiled. There is no one definition or theory that can accurately describe every type of ghost.

The Theories of Ghosts

There are many theories for the existence of ghosts. These theories are based on paranormal and scientific explanations. A few of these theories may seem as inconceivable as the existence of ghosts is to skeptics, but nevertheless, these theories must be recognized as other possibilities. There is no single theory that can adequately account for every type of ghost. Some theories will explain one category of ghost but leave out many other ghost categories. Many of these theories are just as unproven as the existence of ghosts, but the existence of ghosts can only be proven after every alternative possibility has been thoroughly examined.

Apparitions of the Dead:

The most popular theory is that ghosts are the supernatural manifestations of deceased human beings or animals. The apparitions are fully conscious having the same memories and personalities from their former lives. They are almost exactly as they were in life. Apparitions are intelligent, decision-making manifestations capable of expressing feelings and communicating messages to other ghosts and the living. They have the power to manipulate the natural environment such as moving objects, creating sounds, casting shadows, and changing the temperature. Ghosts appear and disappear at will and behave in their own manner. They have their own agenda and communicate with whomever they wish when they feel like interacting. The repeated manifestation of a ghost is classified as a haunting.

Portal (Gateway) Theory:

The portal theory suggests that there are natural occurring doorways that can open up exposing other dimensions to our known reality. These other dimensions can be alternate universes running parallel to our own or they can be dimensions such as a spirit dimension. (The spirit dimension would be a place where souls go after death.) When a dimensional gateway opens, we can see ghosts and view the activities taking place in the spirit world. Some believe that there are triggers that can unlock or open the supernatural gateways. A person in the right place at the right time can open the gateways or reading aloud a passage from a magical book can open a gateway. Others believe that these gateways are randomly occurring phenomena and sometimes a lucky human being is present to witness the thrilling outcome. It's a belief of many cultures that naturally occurring gateways open on Halloween night. On Halloween night, the vale between dimensions becomes so thin that ghosts and other spirits can freely move about in our reality as they wish.

Purgatory:

Purgatory is mostly a religious belief held by some Catholic believers as well as other worldly religious orders. It is based on the belief that when a person dies their soul cannot go directly to Heaven or Hell. The soul must stay in a place called Purgatory until that soul has paid for the sins of their life. Purgatory is also a stage in the transition to afterlife. It is a place where the soul is tormented.

How long a soul must stay in Purgatory depends on each soul and what type of sins were perpetrated in life. Some bad souls will have to stay in purgatory much longer than others and their torment will be much greater. The pain in purgatory can be incredible. The purpose of this intense pain is to purify the soul. Eventually, the soul will be cleansed of sin and will be eligible to be transferred to a higher plane of existence, usually Heaven. Ghosts are seen as souls stuck in Purgatory. Ghosts are in pain, suffering and lost in their own tormented misery. When a ghost has suffered enough pain and torment, their soul will be cleansed of sin and released from Purgatory.

Time Slips:

Time slips are irregular occurrences that somehow permit the past and present to collide at one point allowing individuals in the present to have a glimpse into the past. The past events are seen exactly as they happened. The past places, people, events, and everything else is extremely accurate because, for all intensive purposes, the past event is not an illusion of the past, nor is it a recording of the past, but it is actually the past event taking place as it is happening. This can be confusing because it seems to create a paradox; how can a past event that is many years over be happening in the present? This concept is theoretically possible and revolves around quantum physics. There are people who theorize that time slips can account for some ghost sightings. Instead of seeing a traditional ghost, the witnesses are actually looking at a past event as it unfolds in a time slip. There is no formula for predicting when and where a time slip will occur. Time slips seem to be completely random events that last briefly.

Psychic Prism:

The psychic prism theory suggests that dwellings such as houses can store up psychic energy and then intermittently release that energy throughout the dwelling triggering haunting characteristics. The dwelling theoretically acts as a conductor for the psychic energy. The built up psychic energy flows through the dwelling and prisms into rooms creating what people believe are paranormal events associated with a ghost. The way that dwellings are built can help distribute the psychic energy to different sections of a dwelling. Structures built with spiral or pillar features can create whirlwinds of psychic energy that can pull other psychic energy into the dwelling. There is also a belief that some types of building materials (wood, stone, metal, etc.) used in building a house can be conductors to store psychic energy. The released psychic energy can produce holographic visions, strange shadows or lights, and other characteristics similar to a haunting that can be misconstrued as the activity of a ghost. Of course, this theory does not account for ghosts that appear outside of dwellings.

Telepathy:

Telepathy is the mind-to-mind communication between separate individuals. This type of communication can come in several different forms. One of those is a communication where visual images are sent into another persons mind. These images would be seen not so much as reality is seen, but more like a virtual overlay that merges into the environment. In this theory, people unknowingly transmit a mental image into another person's mind that then see that image and believe it to be a paranormal experience.

Many times people in a haunted area are aware of the fact that the place might be haunted and they have an idea of what type of ghost (appearance, dress, actions) could be seen and experienced. The heightened sense of anticipation might cause a person's psychic abilities to kick on and send a mental image to another person completely at random or unconsciously.

While a controversial theory, it would account for some of the errors that pop up when individuals are describing a ghost's appearance. The errors can be in historic clothing not quite matching a particular time period or certain items such as furniture that were never in the room. It's believed that these errors are because the person unknowingly projecting the image has a picture of how a ghost might look but does not have the historical knowledge to produce an accurate image.

Psychic Echoes and Projections:

Psychic echoes are real sounds and voices from past events that have been recorded onto elements in the natural environment. The sounds are stored up in the environment where they remain dormant until something or someone triggers them to playback. When the sounds playback, they sound exactly like they did when they were recorded.

A projection is basically the same as a psychic echoes except that there is a picture of a past event that can be accompanied with the sound. Both picture and sound can become reordered in the natural environment and play back like a movie when triggered. So witnesses are not actually seeing ghosts, but a recorded experience recorded and played back for them. A projection does not always have sound. Sometimes the projection is only a silent picture.

An unusual aspect of projection playbacks is that sometimes the sounds do not match up correctly with the visuals that witnesses are seeing. It's almost as if both the picture and sound have been successfully recorded in two separate recordings and the recordings are not matching up when a playback is triggered.

The projection theory is another theoretical theory based in quantum physics. A traumatic event occurs releasing a lot of energy which suspends the light particles in the environment until an outside variable in the future triggers them. When triggered, the light particles begin to vibrate in the atmosphere creating a holographic projection of the past event that caused them to become trapped in the environment. Projections need an indoor location so that weather conditions cannot interfere. Because projections consist of vibrating light particles, there could be many individuals in the same room, but only a few could witness the projection based on angle and distance.

Hallucinations:

Hallucinations are the perception of nonexistent objects, people, and/or events. Hallucinations involve seeing, hearing, smelling, tasting, feeling, and experiencing things that are not real, but seem very real to the person having the hallucination. Hallucinations are most often the result of a mental illness, but narcotics can also produce hallucinations.

Skeptics often say that witnesses to the paranormal are not actually seeing ghosts, but experiencing a hallucination. There is a misconception that hallucinations are common. Neurologists can point out, hallucinations are extremely rare and will only happen due to a disorder or from an exposure to narcotics or other hallucinatory substances. The majority of people in this world will never experience a hallucination. There is nothing that can cause different people at the same location over different periods of time from experiencing the same hallucination.

Out of Body Experiences:

An Out of Body Experience (OBE) is a phenomenon in which a person's soul seems to release from their body while they are still alive and healthy. The person is free to travel around outside of their body visiting other places before they have to return to their dormant body. OBE experiences can be mistaken for ghosts because the person's soul can sometimes be seen as an apparition form. The apparition can be solid or transparent and looks and acts similar to the real person. Witnesses report an apparition thinking they had just seen a ghost, but in reality, they have just witnessed an Out of Body Experience. Because the person having the Out of Body Experience is still alive, their apparition will look modern and not dated like most other ghost sightings. They will have modern appearances (clothing, hairstyles, jewelry, etc.).

Human Agents:

Human agents are normal everyday people who unknowingly have a psychic power called Psychokinesis (PK). Psychokinesis is the ability to move or levitate objects by using only mind power. Human agents typically have very fragile emotional states and are usually between the ages of 12 and 24. The agent's emotional problems can include anxiety, hysteria, phobias, and anger or more advanced mental disorders.

Human agents are often blamed for poltergeist cases. The paranormal events begin small with strange scratching noises and household items sliding across the floor. These paranormal events tend to trigger paranoia and fear in the witnesses, one of which is usually the human agent. The human agent is not aware that their own undiagnosed psychic ability is controlling the paranormal events. The paranormal events cause the human agent's emotional tensions to escalate and spiral out of control. Soon it becomes clear that the human agent is the center of all of the activity. Paranormal events will only happen in the presence of the agent and the agent will even begin to predict future paranormal events. It's not that the agent is actually predicting the future; instead, the agent believes in their mind that a paranormal event is about to occur so their unconscious mind takes over and activates the psychokinesis ability. The paranormal activity usually fades when the human agent is treated for their emotional problems or when they reach an age where their hormones do not control their emotional state.

Pranks - Frauds:

It's very easy to fake ghosts and haunts. Tricksters have been doing it since the early 1900's spiritualist movement. Sometimes the person creating a bogus ghost sighting is doing it to see if they can fool the public or trick an experienced parapsychologist. They are doing it just to have fun or to poke fun at the belief in ghosts. There are other people who fake ghosts to make a profit or for a publicity stunt. Financial gain is always a chief motive behind simulating paranormal activity. Frauds have been getting rich for years by duping the general public. For other people, creating a fraud is a way to get attention. Computers, editing software, and cheap electrical equipment enables basically anyone the ability to create very realistic ghosts.

Misinterpretations of Natural Events:

There are numerous natural incidences that are mistaken for paranormal events. It's very important to be aware that sometimes there is a very logical explanation for strange activities being mistaken for a ghost. Animals can get into spaces between walls and create scratching sounds. Old electrical wires can fray and short out causing lights to flicker. Natural house settling can create loud creaking noises and footstep-like sounds. The human eyes can play tricks on a person in dim light. They can see shadows slide through doorways and glimpses of unexplainable figures out of the corner of their eye. The wind whistling through rafters can create a deep moaning sound. Naturally occurring events such as ball lighting or marsh gasses can create odd glowing lights that hover and glide over the countryside. Identifying rational explanations is extremely important.

Dreams and Lucid Dreaming - Nightmares:

Some people have dreams that are so realistic that it is impossible to determine whether what happened was real or just a dream. A lucid dream can make a person feel as if they are paralyzed. They can see strange bright colors and menacing shapes moving around them, but they are powerless to move. Intense emotions rush. The dreamer feels trapped and restrained watching helpless as monstrous faces slide around them. The images seem real. The experiences seem real. The only problem is that the person is actually asleep and nothing that they experienced was real. They were in a state that is referred by parapsychologists as a False Awakening. While the person feels as if they have awaked from sleep, they have only waked inside their dream. Lucid dreaming experiences can be terrifying and lead to serious sleep disorders if they are not dealt with accordingly. Experiencing constant lucid dreams is rare, but it is believed that everyone experiences at least one lucid dream in their lifetime. For obvious reasons, anyone experiencing lucid dreams with nightmare-like effects can mistake their situation for the effects of ghosts and paranormal activity.

Evil Spirits:

Another religious belief is that all ghosts are not actually the souls of the deceased, but are in fact evil spirits masquerading as ghosts so that they can manipulate the living. The evil spirits are not souls of the deceased and have never lived as a human being. They are sometimes referred to as demons. These evil spirits pretend to be friendly, sad, or lonely ghosts so that they can lure the living into a false sense of trust. These evil spirits want to take advantage of the living to control them. They want to create fear and cause harm.

Evil spirits desire that the living will voluntarily communicate with them. They pretend to be a lonely ghost, like the lost ghost of a child. It's much easier for an evil spirit to get a living person to willingly communicate with the ghost of a child because it plays off of the human emotions of compassion and caring for children. These evil spirits are not friendly, lost, or cute. It's all an act that they use. Evil spirits are actually vile, monstrous creatures that want the power to create chaos. The attention that the living give to the evil spirits gives them more power. The more power the evil spirit has, the more influence it can take over the environment. By the time the human beings realize that an evil spirit has tricked them, it's usually too late.

Other Psychic Abilities:

There are many other psychic abilities, some known and some yet to be discovered, that could be a possibility for ghost misinterpretations. Clairvoyance is the extrasensory perception that can manifest in visions of past events. A clairvoyant can go into a location and spontaneously see a vision of things that happened in the past. A clairvoyant can see visions of people and places that are long gone in history. These visions do not always mean that there are ghosts at the location. It's believed by some people that everything that happens in life leaves behind an imprint on the environment. A clairvoyant may simply have the ability to tune into these imprints to receive visions.

Retrocognition is a spontaneous vision of the past. These experiences can manifest to anyone regardless of pervious psychic abilities. Similar to a time slip, retrocognition is a displacement of time allowing an individual a window into the past. Psychic abilities can often be mistaken for ghost sightings simply because the psychic is not fully educated in the mind-body relationship of their psychic abilities. The interpretations of the psychic's manifestations and visions are fundamentally incorrect. The mental pictures of past events and individuals dressed in period clothing seen by the psychic can be past events imprinted on the environment and not necessarily ghosts. There is also the possibility that other psychic abilities, maybe even abilities yet to be discovered, play a role in misinterpretation of ghosts.

The Human Imagination:

Human imagination is sometimes referred to as the "seventh sense." (The five senses being: touch, taste, sight, smell, and hearing; and the sixth sense being certain psychic abilities). Imagination is the key to intelligence. Imagination gives human beings the ability to have visual experiences in the mind. It's the power to be creative and the freedom to realize that there is much more happening in the universe than most people will ever comprehend.

Human imagination plays a large role with ghosts and haunted houses. People will experience (see, hear, feel, smell) paranormal events that never occurred at haunted locations because their mind expected paranormal activity to occur and their imagination simply took over and filled in the blanks. Even in the cases of real ghosts, the human imagination can run rampant in witnesses making them experience all kinds of paranormal activity that never actually happened. Imagination is a powerful tool that can get out of hand when combined with paranormal subjects. If a person thinks that a location is haunted then they will expect a certain amount of paranormal activity to occur. Combine that supernatural awareness with other outside factors that affect the human senses, like not being able to see in the dark or hearing strange noises, and suddenly everything that happens is labeled paranormal. The human imagination causes people to perceive paranormal events that are not real.

There is a flip side to this coin. Some people believe that the human imagination is the reason that people have the ability to see ghosts. There is a belief that the human imagination opens a doorway so that people can become aware of the unseen wonders that surround them. The imagination is acting like a key unlocking the full potential of the human brain's untapped powers. Human beings judge reality on what our body's senses can determine as real. If imagination is truly a seventh human sense then there is a profound possibility that a new chapter of human evolution has yet to be fully realized.

Fear - The Power of Fear:

The power of fear is often underestimated in the case of ghosts. Fear can control and manipulate any situation to become more overblown than the actual reality of the situation. A person who believes they are living in a house with a ghost is programmed to believe that they will experience certain "ghostly" activity: doors opening and closing, strange noises, unexplained footsteps, apparitions, etc. People can see or hear just about anything when they expect to run into ghosts.

After fear has taken control, just about any event, no matter how logical the explanation, becomes something supernatural. Even people who live with real ghosts can fall into this trap. If someone is living with a ghost and their gold fish happens to die that doesn't mean that the ghost killed the fish, but that's often what people will believe. Fear causes people to believe everyday happenings, incidents that take place to millions of people every day, are supernatural simply because of a ghost. A light bulb burns out, "It's the ghost!" The basement floods, "It's the ghost!" Fear generates an irrational panic that must be controlled otherwise everything will be perceived as a supernatural event.

Fear is a natural human emotion. It is a survival instinct. Human beings fear the unknown to keep us safe and out of harms way. The cycle of fearing ghosts can be broken through education and understanding. The more a person learns and understands about ghosts, the less that person will fear them. This of course does not mean letting your guard down around ghosts or trying to befriend every ghost. Caution is a wise man's greatest virtue. When it comes to ghosts, you don't have to be afraid, but always put safety first.

The Nature of a Ghost

The nature or attitude of a ghost can be benevolent, malevolent, or neutral. There is a common misconception that ghosts are evil and violent beings. A ghost is only as good or evil as they were while alive. The large majority of ghosts are equivalent to an average everyday person. Each ghost has a unique personality filled with ordinary personal habits, constant behaviors, and varying degrees of temperament. A ghost is not good or evil by nature. A basic ghost is not manifesting to create good deeds and peace on earth, but it also does not have malicious intent, hatred, or contempt for the living.

The depiction of a devilish ghost comes mainly from fictional Hollywood movies and does not represent the reality of most common ghosts. Ghosts do not manifest for the sole purpose of creating harm, misfortune, and evil deeds. A common ghost is a victim of a tragic situation. Typically, ghosts are sad, lonely, depressed, and basically pathetic beings of circumstance. A common ghost is way too busy brooding in their own self-misery to meddle in the affairs of the living. A lot of ghosts do not even have the power to cause harm. Many ghosts appear in the physical realm continuously reenacting events from their lifetime seemingly unaware of the world working around them. There are certain ghosts that have been seen numerous times over hundreds years that have never once caused harm. Several types of ghosts seem completely oblivious to the presence of living people. These ghosts continue to act out daily routines as if they had never died. The recurring ghost is, in essence, "doing it's own thing" while it either refuses to or is unable to acknowledge the existence of the living.

There are individuals teaching and preaching that all ghosts, regardless of the circumstance, are hateful and wicked, or are servants of Satan; the Christian symbol of ultimate evil. Most of these false perceptions are derived from personal opinions and misinterpretations of religious scriptures. These false ghost perceptions have very little to do with scientific research, real experiences, or actual facts. Common ghosts are not manifestations of evil and ghosts are not created nor controlled by demonic forces. The fact is that most ghosts are harmless and in some cases, such as a compassionate presence ghost or an elusive mystery ghost (both of which you will read about later), actually help the living. Ghosts have been known to provide important information prior to disastrous events that actually save human lives - not exactly a demonic characteristic. Ghosts can help people if they choose to help.

Ghosts are often depicted as stereotypical villains - evil, malicious, and with an utter contempt for human life. Ghosts are feared and demonized because there is an unknown inherent danger with encountering a ghost. A ghost will always have the advantage in an encounter. Ghosts have supernatural abilities that give them an upper hand. They can see a person when the person cannot see them. They can travel through solid objects like walls or hover above a room. They can hear a private conversation. Until the identity of the ghost is discovered, it is very hard to judge what types of habits the ghost is likely to conduct. Encountering a ghost is like running into a stranger on the street.

A ghost may be benevolent, malevolent, or neutral, but they are not necessarily evil or wicked simply because they are a ghost. This is not saying that a ghost cannot be malicious. Maximum caution should always be used when encountering any ghosts. In very rare circumstances, a ghost can attempt to cause harm to a living person. There are types of ghosts, such as the ghost of murderers, which might want to continue their murderous ways in the afterlife. It is estimated that less than 1% of all ghosts harbor malicious intent for the living. These ghosts are hateful in death because they were hateful in life.

Ghosts can use their supernatural abilities to scare and torment the living. Ghostly abuse may also include violent activities such as biting, slapping, and pushing. There has never been a case documented of a ghost physically murdering a living person, but many people have attributed untimely deaths to the supernatural workings of a ghost. Many human injuries sustained during ghost encounters are a direct result of fear causing the person to fall down or collide with objects during their hasty retreat.

Every single person has the potential to become dangerous or violent in the right situation; therefore every ghost, even a gentle ghost, has the potential to become dangerous or violent in the right circumstances. A ghost that was not violent in life and not violent in death, as a ghost, can become irritated to the point where that ghost might shove or strike a living person out of pure frustration. It's the loss of control that happens in a single regrettable moment. If ghosts are no different from people in how they act, then it must be understood that a ghost has the potential to lose control too.

The belief that ghosts of the dead are malevolent is not a new theory. Traditionally in the English society, the dead are buried by their relatives in cemeteries, which are essentially cities of the dead physically separated from the reality of the living. Cemeteries are separate from the living because it was believed that ghosts could cause harm or influence people in a negative manner. It was also believed that a person that was not buried in holy ground would come back as a ghost to haunt and attack the living. Ghosts were seen as powerful and dangerous.

Some ghosts are territorial and do not like it when their resting place is disturbed. These ghosts will act out and cause problems for people who they feel are infringing on their personal space. This type of ghost will begin its haunt by creating subtle hints for the living to leave. If its early warnings are not heeded, the ghost will escalate its activity to the point where it may be potentially harmful to the living. These ghosts will stop their activity when they are left alone.

Caution should be used in all cases were a ghost could be present, especially when there are children involved. The odds are extremely rare that a ghost will attempt to create harm, but percentages are not a good enough reason to leave one's own personal protection or a child's protection to chance. Ghosts should be kept at a distance. A ghost should not be communicated with on a regular basis. Ghosts should not be summoned or used for the benefit of the living. They should not be befriended or regarded as a companion. Ghosts are people who are no longer alive and they should not be mingling with the living. It is very important that people understand that ghosts are supernatural beings capable of a wide range of paranormal activity, some of which might be fashioned for malicious intent.

Sugar, Spice and Ectoplasm…

Living beings have organic bodies made up of flesh and blood. These bodies consist of structured organs that produce and process fluids keeping the body alive and functioning properly. Organic bodies also provide a housing structure for the electrically functioning brain and nervous systems. When the human body dies, the organic structure (flesh, organs, tissue, bones) begins to decay immediately. This process is fulfilling the scientific law that states, "Energy cannot be created nor destroyed. Energy can only be transformed from one form of energy into another form of energy."

The organic matter of the human body decomposes and transforms into a new form of energy, but what happens to the electrical impulses centered in the human brain and nervous system? No scientist has absolutely determined what happens to this electrical energy at the point of death. According to the rule of science, the electrical energy flowing through a living creature cannot simply fade out of existence. That electric energy must be transformed into a new form of energy, which means that it still exists after death, but in a different form.

Many parapsychologists know that when ghosts are present there are abnormal electro-magnetic fields. The same EMF (electro-magnetic fields) that surrounds every living creature is also detectable in the presence of ghosts. The EMF fields that accompany ghosts are usually strong enough to interfere with manmade electrical devices. (Television sets turn on and off. Radio stations change. Computer equipment will stop working.) The levels of static electricity will also rise in haunted environments. Almost everything touched will burst with a static charge. Even the air itself will become modified in the presence of a ghost. The temperature will change, sometimes becoming much colder (or hotter) than the rest of the area for no apparent reason. The strange temperature spots can vary as much as ten or more degrees from the rest of the area. Air ion counters will also reveal whether or not ions in the air are charged more than normal.

Ghosts seem to function much like a battery. When the ghosts are full of energy, they are capable of a variety of supernatural abilities such as moving objects, interfering with electrical appliances, mimicking sounds and voices, manipulating the physical environment by creating shadows and clouds, and appearing as apparitions. However, as the ghost uses its energy, it becomes drained like a used battery. As the ghost's energy weakens, so do their supernatural powers. A ghost will rest when its energy levels are exhausted until its' used up energies have been replenished - then the haunting process can start over again.

Every individual ghost will have different energy levels and will utilize their energy in different ways. It depends on the particular ghost and the situations surrounding each haunting. Some ghosts seem to have very limited energy levels and will only be able to conduct a restricted amount of supernatural abilities while other ghosts seem to have a boundless amount of energy that allows them to produce supernatural abilities seemingly on command at nearly any time. The reason for the varying degrees of power between different ghosts is unknown. There are theories that suggest the possibility that certain locations in the natural environment provide a ghost with additional power. The earth releases invisible energies that spiral up as a type of energy vortex. A ghost that happens to be close to one of these energy vortexes can use that natural energy to fuel its own powers. In this theory, ghosts are everywhere on earth, but the living can only experience the ghosts that are in close proximity to these natural springs of supernatural energy.

Ghosts are also said to produce a substance called ectoplasm. Ectoplasm is a paranormal residue that oozes and materializes from people or objects after contact with a ghost. Ectoplasm can also be in the form of mists, clouds, and liquids. It is often depicted as a white, milky-colored substance. Ectoplasm is supposedly an energized blanket of moisture that travels in the air and is said to move and twist like it has a mind of its own. Sometimes photographs can show evidence of ectoplasm that was not visible to the human eye at the time the photographs were taken. In the late nineteenth century, fraudulent psychics and mediums duped hundreds of people by creating their own ectoplasm by mixing soap, gelatin, and egg whites together. Despite the fact that frauds took advantage of ectoplasm, it does not discourage the belief that ectoplasm exists. Many people who come into contact with ghosts claim to see strange white twisting figures around the apparition and smell a distinct ozone smell common in reports of ectoplasm. (The ozone smell is consistent with electrical charges and static bursts of electricity.)

There are numerous mysteries, inconsistencies, and paradoxes when dealing with the "bodies" of ghosts. They do not have real physical bodies to block light yet they may still cast a shadow. They can move through a room and leave behind a vapor trail or mist. A ghost can appear with a lifelike body and then walk right through a solid wall. There are many enigmas circling ghosts that are yet to be fully understood.

The Energy of Ghosts

Energy is the capacity to do work. Objects in motion need energy to power the action. A person walking down the street, a basketball bouncing, and the moon orbiting the earth are all examples of objects in motion using energy. Without energy, there cannot be movement. Energy comes in many different forms from chemical, thermal (heat), gravitational, nuclear, electrical, magnetic, and electromagnetic. The two types of energy that give all objects motion are potential and kinetic energy. Potential energy is stored energy while kinetic energy is energy performing an action. A waterfall is an example of both potential and kinetic energy at work. At the top of a waterfall, the water has potential energy. As the water falls over the waterfall, the potential energy is transformed into kinetic energy.

A ghost operates through electromagnetic fields. It is known that ghosts affect electromagnetic fields because it can be registered with EMF (electro-magnetic field) detectors, which can record the fluctuations of natural EMF fields when ghosts are present. A ghost will affect electrical equipment such as computers, cell phones, and television sets by overpowering their signals and sensitive circuits with unnaturally high EMF fields. High EMF fields can damage sensitive electrical instruments.

The human body stores potential energy inside the muscles. The potential energy is transformed into kinetic energy as a person walks to the refrigerator or runs a marathon. Ghosts essentially operate in basically the same way. A ghost must store energy until it wants to move or create an action. Then the potential energy (stored) is transformed to kinetic energy (motion). It is believed by some that a ghost could not store energy because it does not have a form (or body), but that is not true because energy does not need a container. A solar flare, energy released from the Sun, is a mass of invisible energy moving across space.

Solar flares are very destructive to electrical equipment because they release large amounts of energy. Solar flares release much more energy than a single ghost, but the amount of energy is irrelevant. It's the effects that are important. Ghosts and solar flares act very similar. Both ghosts and solar flares are forms of invisible energy that release electromagnetic energy. Ghosts and solar flares disrupt sensitive electrical equipment. Researchers who study ghosts and solar flares tend to use similar tools like x-ray equipment to detect gamma rays or radio and radiation detection equipment capable of monitoring the amounts of energy in the environment.

Paranormal researchers believe that ghosts steal energy from outside sources and store it like a battery until it is ready to use the energy. When ghosts are present, there are abnormal fluctuations in electrical systems. In haunted houses fuses burn out regularly, power surges go off, and the lights dims as if the electricity is being drained from the power supply. Ghost hunters often have flashlights, cameras, and other electrical equipment stop working in the field for no reason. The batteries of the flashlights and cameras go completely dead even when brand new batteries are used. No one can explain how ghosts draw the energy from electrical equipment.

Ghosts use stored energy to move, create sounds, appear as apparitions, etc. The more activity that a ghost conducts the more energy it will expend. Once a ghost has depleted its' stored energy, it must replenish its energy supply by resting. Paranormal studies show that a ghost will seem to go dormant after a period of high paranormal activity. It's not that the ghost has left or disappeared, but that the ghost used up its stored energy and simply cannot do any more. The ghost will rest until it has stored up enough new energy to begin the paranormal cycle again.

Ghosts draw energy from outside sources seemingly effortlessly. It is like the ghost is acting as a magnet drawing energy from anything that the ghost comes in contact with that has an energy source. A ghost also seems to draw heat energy from the environment. In many haunted houses, small areas or entire rooms will become very cold when a ghost is present. The ghost could be drawing the heat energy from the atmosphere leaving behind colder surroundings.

A ghost produces unexplained phenomena by using stored energy to effect the environment. The human eye cannot see these energy discharges, but the energy can be measured with scientific equipment and photographed with cameras. Photographs taken at haunted houses often show ghostly lights, energy anomalies, plasma fields, vortexes, orbs, and other strange twisting light phenomena. Cameras can catch what the human eye cannot see because a camera works on a different light spectrum. All forms of energy are visible in the correct light spectrum. X-rays are visible in the x-ray spectrum. Infrared light is visible in the infrared spectrum. Even heat can be seen with thermal imaging equipment.

It is important to understand how ghosts work physically because it is the foundation for its' paranormal activity. It is also important because most skeptics believe that ghosts work outside the rules of science. Skeptics believe that ghosts cannot be real because there very existence goes against the laws of science while the opposite is actually true. The more that ghosts are studied the more accurate information is discovered that suggests that ghosts work within the boundaries and laws of science. Ghosts are creatures of energy that store potential energy and use kinetic energy just as science dictates. The principle that ghosts cannot exist because they do not follow the rules of science is based on false personal beliefs and scientific misinterpretation.

How Ghosts Communicate

To communicate with ghosts, there are several things that the living must first understand. When it comes to communication, ghosts are not like the living. Ghosts will not always be able to carry on a spoken conversation to express their thoughts and feelings. However, communication is more than just spoken words and phrases. Each ghost will communicate in its own unique way. They will use available methods that express their true sentiments and attract the most attention. Ghostly communication can be made through visions, emotions, noises, or smells.

A major problem with many people who study the paranormal is that they do not see the big picture when it comes to communicating with ghosts. Human beings communicate to each other mainly through language, but even without a voice, there are endless ways to communicate with another person; from complex hand jesters like sign language to the small expression on a person's face. People who study ghosts must first understand that ghosts can communicate without ever speaking a word. A ghost's conscious interactions are a new language and a new form of unique communication.

Everything that a ghost does is a method of communication. The way a ghost appears, the noises that a ghost makes, the types of fragrances that a ghost leaves behind, the places that a ghost haunts most frequently, and the items that a ghost chooses to move are all ways for a ghost to communicate.

When an apparition is seen, communication might be as simple as a short glance or acknowledgement through eye contact. Communication can be the direction in which a ghost walks. The ghost might be trying to get the witness to follow it.

When a ghost knocks on the walls, it is trying to draw attention to itself and communicate with the living. The rapping is basically a form of ghostly Morse code. The ghost wants to be noticed because it is trying to express a thought or feeling but doesn't have the ability to communicate normally.

Even the way a ghost looks to a witness is a form of communication. A ghost's appearance (clothing, hair style, shoes) is visual communication to the witness that the ghost is from a specific time period. If a ghost has a deep scar on the side of its face, that tells the witness that the ghost was injured in life. If a ghost manifests without an arm, that is a way of communicating that it may be looking for its missing arm. If a ghost appears carrying a book, witnesses should realize that the book contains some sort of significance to that ghost.

When a ghost only appears one time a year in one specific location, that ghost is communicating with the intent of bringing attention to the importance of that date, time, and location. Appearing only one time a year is that ghost's way of communicating. The day, time, and location where ghosts manifest are extremely meaningful to each particular specter. These details are important because they provide clues into the background of the ghost.

It may seem ironic, but ghosts are not always good at ghostly communication. Many ghosts do not seem to know how to communicate as ghosts. They do things that do not seem to have any rational meaning like banging on walls, slamming doors, or shrieking in the middle of the night. They are experimenting with different ways of communicating. People who study ghosts have to understand that some ghosts might not be aware of what types of communication are available to them. A ghost who bangs on the walls constantly might be doing that because they don't know what else to do to get attention. The ghost might want to reach out and communicate, but in their present situation they do not know how to communicate. Ghosts may become frustrated and confused. Ghosts will do whatever is in their power to get attention and that's why all ghostly activity should be seen as a method of communication.

Understanding the Cause, Meaning, and Origin

Understanding the cause, meaning, and origin of a ghost is vital to figuring out the character and unique habits of that ghost. The cause, meaning, and origin is basically the "who, what, and why" of a ghost. To understand why a ghost manifests with certain ghostly characteristics, one must examine the whole story of the ghost; from the life of the person to the event that caused their death and how they act in their afterlife. All of the information gathered about a ghost is essential to knowledgably comprehending that ghost. Ghosts are part of a large paranormal puzzle. Each piece of the puzzle must be thoroughly examined and learned to develop a profile.

The Cause:

The cause is the event that triggers a ghost to be born. The vast majority of the ghosts haunting the world are created by the direct result of a sudden, violent and unexpected death. The horrible events that can cause sudden death could be just about anything; from being shot during a battle, killed in an automobile accident, sustaining a fatal sports injury, or getting hit by a bus while crossing the street. The cause of a ghost is the instant moment where life has been abruptly taken. The cause is only the first piece of the paranormal puzzle, but it is the beginning of a ghost.

The Meaning:

The meaning of a ghost is the internal and external reasons that a ghost manifests. The cause creates the reason that a person dies and the meaning is why that person is now a ghost. There are internal and external factors that decide whether a ghost will haunt. The internal reasons arise when ghosts refuse to let go of their past life. There is an underlying psychological reason inside the ghost causing it to intentionally exist as a ghost. The ghost's own internal emotions are the root of the problems. The ghost feels that their life is not yet finished. Internal reasons are profound and will trouble a ghost enough to keep them haunting.

There are also external reasons that trap unwilling ghosts. A violent automobile accident can be so powerful that it "burns" the awful accident into the natural environment. The ghost becomes stuck in a recurring nightmare. These ghosts, through no fault of their own, are trapped by their external circumstances. They manifest because they do not have any other choice.

The Origin:

The origin is the past personality and history of the individual who is now a ghost. Before the individual was a ghost, they were a living breathing person. The personality of an individual and the events going on in their lifetime are key ingredients that make up the meaning behind a ghost. A person's unique behaviors, traits, and qualities develop their personality. A strong personality and daily lifetime events combine to help build the foundations for a ghost. For example, if a young man is getting married, working at a great job, in the process of buying a new home, and basically has everything in the world going his way then is suddenly killed in a freak accident, this could be the formula to create a ghost. There is nothing absolute that says this man will definitely become a ghost because his life was cut short, but the man's lifestyle and personality can directly support whether or not he becomes a ghost. If this man does become a ghost then his life experience will directly assist what he does as a ghost. The man's ghost might appear searching for his wife, or appear at his workplace, or maybe even manifest standing in front of the house he was to buy. The way that a ghost will act is a direct result of the character of the person and the life that they lived.

The entire representation of the cause, meaning, and origin make up a complete spirit profile of a ghost. This spirit profile can be used to determine when and where a particular ghost will manifest and what type of paranormal activity it will conduct. When the whole picture of a ghost is closely examined, there is almost always a common blueprint that emerges for creating a ghost. The cause is almost certainly a sudden and violent event that takes a person's life unexpectedly. The meaning revolves around the feelings of confusion, loss, and the desire to regain a past life. Lastly, the origin is typically an individual with a strong personality and high emotions that bind them to life. When death comes, these people refuse to give up on their life. Certain elements combine in just the right way and a ghost is created. Most ghosts will follow this simple pattern, but every ghost is different and there is always an oddball ghost that fails to fit into any of the common ghost molds. Each ghost is unique and mysterious and should be studied with respect and wisdom.

The Time is Short

The average ghost sighting will last for less than ten seconds. That is only a minuscule amount of precious time. During that time, most people freeze up. Witnesses are terrified and in shock. In most ghost sightings, the experience is wasted. No one is ever prepared to see a ghost. Even parapsychologists and ghost hunters who are in the field looking for ghosts are not prepared when it actually happens. Fear and confusion are normal feelings for a witness to have when face to face with a ghost. It is important for a witness to take full advantage of the time to fully observe and study the ghost's description. The ghost's appearance, attitude, and actions can help determine the type of ghost.

Eyewitness descriptions are a double-edged sword. The problem with eyewitness accounts is that they are hardly ever accurate. The ability to perceive and remember accurately is not as reliable as people think. People see things from their own perspective, which will influence their assessment of the experience. Ten witnesses can be present to see the same ghost and yet each witness will give a different description of the event. Sometimes the descriptions can be complete opposites. There are paranormal researchers that believe that the different descriptions are because the ghost is showing itself differently to each witness, but law institute studies on eyewitnesses show serious faults in that theory.

In tests done at Harvard and Yale, subjects were submitted to false crimes lasting a few seconds. The subjects were then asked to describe the perpetrator. The results were amazing with all the subjects swearing to different depictions of the same criminal. Some subjects gave the criminal a mustache, some a beard, while others said no facial hair. This same type of inconsistency went on for every characteristic proving that what the eyes see is not always accurate.

It is important not to give too much credibility to varying eyewitness descriptions of a ghost. The inaccuracies are not necessarily intentional and should not be regarded as lying, but outside factors have to be taken into account with eyewitness descriptions. How afraid the witnesses were at the time of the sighting, how far away from the ghosts they were at the time, how long the sighting lasted, if the witnesses had impaired perceptions such as not wearing their glasses or having an earring aid.

Most people who see a ghost are not expecting to see a ghost and in some cases do not even realize that they have seen a ghost until after the experience is over. Ghost sightings happen so fast that it is almost impossible for the witness to do the things that should be done, like examining the ghost. Eyewitnesses should try to examine the ghost. (Is the ghost male or female, what type of clothing is it wearing, does the ghost have any distinguishing features, etc.) It is important for a witness to keep an eye on the ghost until it disappears from sight.

When a ghost sighing is over, the witness should immediately sit down and write out exactly what happened. The witness should detail what they saw, heard, smelled, and felt as well as any other abnormal occurrences that happened before, during, or after the sighting. It is also a good idea to draw pictures and keep detailed notes while the experience is still fresh. If a witness waits too long before putting their experience down on paper, there is a chance that it will be contaminated by false memories and the minds own power of persuasion. If a witness thinks about their experience too much, they will begin to add details to their memory of things that were not there or did not happen. The witness's prior expectations will start to cloud the true memory.

The effect of seeing a ghost can be a life-changing experience. Those who have been lucky enough to see a ghost will relive the experience for the rest of their lives. The opportunity to observe a ghost is a once in a lifetime event and should be treated as a great chance to get a firsthand look into the world of the supernatural.

An Examination of Haunted Houses

Any type of building can become haunted, but haunted houses are the most common type of haunted structure. A haunted house is a dwelling inhabited by one or many ghosts. These houses often exhibit many types of paranormal activity such as moving objects, unexplainable noises, strange lights, apparitions, etc. Most haunted houses are not dangerous environments to live in, but they can be extremely frightening for people who are not prepared to experience ghosts. There are many different reasons why ghosts haunt houses. Some ghosts may have lived at the same residence for their entire lives and do not want to leave it after their death. Other haunted houses are the scene of violent murders and other terrible disasters. Ghosts typically haunt places that have a connection to their past life.

Houses are property and protection. People are supposed to feel a sense of security locked inside their own home. Houses are supposed to be a safe haven where people can live peacefully, tucked away from the hostile outside world. People love their homes. Houses are a representation of the owners. Homeowners buy furniture and decorate their homes to fit their own personal styles and to make the house feel like it is theirs.

When a ghost haunts a house, the dwelling ceases to feel like a safe place because the presence of a ghost creates a violation of privacy and a loss of security. A haunted house can feel like a worthless prison to the owners. The home no longer belongs to the living, but to the ghosts haunting it. The homeowners live in constant fear of the unknown. They do not know what will happen next and they do not understand what is happening to their home. Most ghosts can live peacefully with the living, but for the most part, the living does not want to share their home with the dead.

If a person is living inside a haunted house the, best thing they can do is document the haunting activity. They need to write down everything that happens inside the house. Keep notes on the date, time, and locations of every paranormal event that occurs inside the house. They can also take photographs and use video cameras to look for any abnormal photographic or video distortions. The paranormal activity of haunted houses tends to be concentrated in a few specific locations throughout the house. Once the prime areas have been discovered, center the search for ghostly evidence in those areas. It is also a good idea to do background research on the house to look for any evidence of a death or murder. Gathering information and evidence can help the owners of a haunted house have a better understanding of what type of ghost they are dealing with and what, if anything, can be done about the haunting.

Class 1: The Basic Haunting

A basic haunting involves a single ghost haunting a single house. These are the most common of all haunted houses. The ghost is usually a previous owner who died inside the home or on the grounds. The ghost's death did not have to involve anything violent, sudden, or unusual. The person might have lived a long full life and died quietly of natural causes.

A basic haunting involves all of the characteristics of a common ghost such as strange noises and lights, moving objects, apparition manifestations, etc. The ghost is usually not angry or bitter, but seems to be quiet, peaceful, and content to remain in their home after death. They continue to conduct their daily routines as if they had not died. These ghosts are intelligent and curious beings. They do not try to scare people out of their home, but they will protect and watch over their property against anyone who does not respect it. These ghosts are the basic “bump in the night” ghosts. They can be heard, seen, and felt. The owners of the house will know that there is a ghost present, but do not necessarily feel threatened or afraid of the ghost. There is no way to get rid of these types of ghosts and they will continue to haunt for as long as they want.

Class 2: Multiple Haunting

A multiple haunting is one step up from the basic haunted house. The main difference between the two is that basic haunts only have one ghost and multiple haunts have two or more ghosts haunting the same location. The ghosts in a multiple haunt do not have to be related to each other and they do not have to be from the same time period. The different ghosts seem to be sharing the dwelling and cohabitating. Each ghost will have a unique personality. Each ghost will also have a separate cause, meaning, and origin. The ghosts work independently from one another and can even seem to aggravate each other at times. Again, there is no way to get rid of these ghosts and they will continue to haunt for as long as they want.

Class 3: Sacred Ground Haunting

Houses built on holy or sacred ground often create a hot spot for ghostly activity. The sacred locations can be old graveyards, cemeteries, churches, ancient burial grounds, ceremonial buildings, worship altars, and sites of religious practices. At the time of a home's construction, it is not always known by the builders that the location was previously used for religious practices. In other cases, the builders might know exactly what they are doing when they construct a home over consecrated ground. In some grisly practices, entire graveyards are moved to new locations to permit the land developers to build middleclass housing subdivisions. The corpses are dug up and relocated to a new cemetery. In these situations, the deceased have been moved, but their ghosts can stay behind and haunt the location of the old graveyard and any building that is built on the site. Sometimes these religious locations were haunted even before any buildings were erected. The ghosts just move into the newly built homes and continue to haunt. The only way to stop these types of haunts is to tear down the homes or other buildings that have been built to let the ghosts have their place of rest.

Class 4: Grasping Vines Haunting

A grasping vines haunted house consists of a single structure, or source house, that branches out to nearby homes like vines growing out to take over the other houses. The ghostly activity will be weaker as the homes get further away from the source house. Homeowners in these situations do not always know that their neighbors are having the same types of supernatural problems because ghosts are the kind of stuff that people usually keep to themselves. Even neighbors who do talk about their similar experiences might not realize that their homes are connected by one main source house. In grasping vine cases, if the source house is eliminated then all of the paranormal activity in the nearby locations will dissipate. Taking the source house out is like breaking a link in a chain.

Class 5: Buried Inside Haunting

A home that has a dead body buried inside it or on the grounds has a very good chance of becoming haunted. The deceased body or bodies might have been secretly placed inside the house to cover up a murder. Murder victims have been sealed up inside walls, placed under floorboards, and buried in basements. Murder is not always the cause in this type of haunt. In past centuries, people who died during the winter when weather was too bad to carry bodies dozens of miles to the nearest town would be buried inside the home until spring. In many cases, the deceased were not dug up and the bodies were left buried inside the home.

The bodies left inside a home can stir up a haunting. These types of haunts can involve both people and animals. Animals are actually more common because they can climb between walls and become trapped and die where the living cannot find them. The bodies of deceased people and animals are usually discovered when homes are undergoing renovation. Once the body has been discovered, it can be laid to rest in an appropriate manner and the ghost may stop haunting the location.

Class 6: Abnormal Anomaly Haunting

There are houses that exhibit all the characteristics of a common haunted house but have no ghosts inside. Instead, the house is located where natural earth energies are being released into the environment. These earth energies can come up through the ground from deep inside the earth in the form of energy vortexes and natural energy springs. The built up energies are electro-magnetically charged and cause the environment to show signs of a false haunting.

Paranormal researchers will argue whether or not any real ghosts have to be present in these types of haunted houses. One side will argue that there are not any ghosts involved and that the natural earth energy is solely responsible for the haunting. The other side will argue that while these energies are the main source of the haunting, there are still some ghosts present. Some paranormal researchers believe that ghosts and other supernatural entities are drawn to locations where electromagnetic energies are being released from the earth.

Abnormal anomalies like energy vortexes and energy springs will run in cycles. The electromagnetic energies inside the earth build up over time until they reach a pressure point where they then erupt from deep inside the earth's crust. The energies are invisible, but they are powerful enough to disrupt electronic communications and cause compasses to spin out of whack. There is no way to stop this haunting because there is no way to cap or divert the energy away from the house.

Class 7: The Tragedy Haunting

Tragedy leaves behind ghosts. Catastrophic events that result in loss of life are common causes for haunted locations. These horrible events can be murder scenes or places where disastrous accidents occurred such as a car or plane crash that has taken the lives of numerous individuals. Sudden and tragic events burn the natural environment where they happen leaving behind a haunting. These haunted locations can be inside or outside a dwelling and multiple ghosts can haunt them. The ghosts of a tragic haunt are usually very sad entities that are seeking ways to express their feelings to the living. These ghosts exhibit all of the typical haunting characteristics. There is nothing that can be done by the living to get rid of these ghosts. Only these souls can work out their problems in their own way and time.

Class 8: Living House Haunting

The living house haunting is the most radical theory for haunted houses. The premise is that a person has died and their ghost departs from its fleshy body container and uses the structure of its home as a new material container. Instead of freely haunting the house, the ghost actually joins with it. A human body is made up of organic material just like a building. The process is similar to a possession, but instead of a human, it is the dwelling that becomes possessed. Using this method, the ghost can take full control of the structure.

In metaphorical terms, the windows of the house become the ghost's new eyes. The electrical systems that run throughout the home become the ghost's nervous system. The walls of the house become the ghost's skin. Everything inside the structure functions as one complete being. When a ghost takes control of a house, the dwelling itself seems to become alive. Everything about the house will change. The rooms will darken and feel less friendly. Visitors will feel like they are constantly being watched. The air inside the house becomes heavy and stale. Even the water will taste different.

In many of these cases, witnesses report seeing blood dripping from the walls, ceiling, and staircases that later disappear without a trace. Some people believe this is the ghost trying to frighten people away from the house or warn them that bad things are about to happen. However, there is another hypothesis suggesting that the blood is just another piece of evidence proving the ghost is trying to physically join with the house. The blood is a paranormal illusion created by the past memories of the ghost. The ghost remembers what it was like to be alive and is trying to use the house to feel that way again.

There is a bad aspect to this type of haunting that is not experienced in a common haunting. When a ghost joins with a house, they seem to lose part of their own personality. The ghost changes its normal behavior. This could be because the ghost is now living in a different existence. It is no longer human and it is no longer a ghost. The ghost becomes something else that now has a different perspective, different driving factors, and different motivations. This is not a common type of haunting and should not be treated as a common haunting.

Ghosts also seem to lose some of their humanity when going through the drastic changes of joining with a house. Do not underestimate the supernatural powers of a ghost working through a house. In this situation, the ghost has total control over everything that occurs inside the house. They can become dangerous and unpredictable. The houses normal reality has been replaced with supernatural laws. This is a condition where the house can go insane. There is almost nothing, short of demolishing the house, that can be done to stop this haunting.

Twenty Questions

Q: There was a double murder in my house many years ago. I feel that those murder victims are now haunting my house. Are those ghosts going to hurt someone in my family?
A: It is very common for the ghosts of murder victims to haunt the scene of their death. These ghosts almost never commit any violent activity. The ghosts were the victims of a senseless crime. They are trapped and suffering and are not seeking to inflict pain and suffering on the living. You should never let your guard down around any ghost, but you should not have any problems with these ghosts becoming violent.

Q: How can I get rid of the ghost inside my house?
A: I don't like to give bad news, but there is not one proven method to force a ghost out of a house. Ghosts haunt places regardless of the living. They, typically, were there first and will be there long after the living has left. There are numerous charms, home remedies, and religious rituals that are supposed to exorcise ghosts. Methods aimed at getting rid of ghosts will either fail to work, work for a very short period of time, or make the haunting worse.

Q: One room in my house is haunted. The room is used as a spare bedroom, but everyone who sleeps there has terrible nightmares involving a woman being strangled. What does this mean and should we be afraid of that room?
A: It is a very good possibility that the people who sleep in this room are experiencing a recurring dream of an event that took place inside that room. It is thought that ghosts can affect a person's dreams, but in this case, there might not even be a ghost. There is a theory that horrible events leave behind powerful traces of psychic energies. It could be that these energies are interfering with normal dream patterns. It is also possible that a ghost (probably the woman

who was strangled) is haunting that room and showing people her fate through dreams. Search for evidence to determine if a murder occurred in the house by looking at old newspaper clippings at the library or ask neighbors. Keep in mind that the murder might be unsolved. The woman's body might have been dumped in a secluded area away from the house. In this case, the ghost might be trying to reach out and show the living how she was murdered or who murdered her.

Q: My house is built on an area where American Indians use to live. The house is haunted and many of my neighbor's houses are also haunted. Is there a connection between the haunted houses and the ground used by the Indians?
A: The connection is a possibility, but it is not because there is anything special about the spiritual or religious practices of the American Indians. Ghosts are found in every culture throughout the world both past and present. Conduct research. There might be a link traced back to the American Indians. Maybe there was a massive battle in that area or maybe the area was used as a holy or burial ground. There is also the possibility that one of the houses in the area is a source house for the rest of the haunted houses. The ghosts inside the source house are branching out and infecting nearby homes. To find the source house, take a map of the area and circle all of the houses in the neighborhood that are having ghost problems. The source house will be in the center of the affected homes. Finding the source house is the first step to understanding the ghosts.

Q: I noticed strange things showed up on films of family events that I videotaped at my house. I thought the video camera was defective so I bought a brand new digital video camera, but that did not help. I record strange lights and shadows that are not visible to anyone at the time. I am now also hearing what sounds like unidentifiable voices in the background of my tapes. What is happening?
A: These are good signs of a haunted house. Paranormal investigators interpret strange lights and abnormal phenomena as proof of a ghost. Continue to shoot more video and take lots of photographs. There are also experiments that can be done like leaving the video camera recording in empty rooms to attempt to

record paranormal activity. Try to decipher the strange voices on the videotape. The voice of a ghost can be recorded on any type of device that records audio. Keep an eye out for any other ghostly activity. Though, it is not completely uncommon to have a ghost that does not disturb the living. In some cases, like this one, it is possible that the ghost could have gone undetected except for the accidental recordings. This does sound like evidence of a ghost, but more evidence should be gathered before any conclusions are made.

Q: I have been living with a ghost for several months. The ghost was not doing anything threatening, but I felt that it would be in my family's best interest to bring in a person who claimed to be able to "cleanse" my house of this ghost. The cleansing ritual seems to have backfired and the ghost's activity has increased dramatically. It is now very hard to live in the house. Is there anything that I can do?
A: First, do not bring in anyone else to "cleanse" your house again. (For those who do not know, "cleansing" is a term used by psychics who claim to be able to get rid of ghosts by performing a ritual.) The big problem with cleansing is that it does not work and often backfires because it can upset the ghost. The irritated ghost has a "how dare you try to throw me out of my home" mentality.

This may sound strange, but there are a couple options in this case. Try talking to the ghost. Simply walk into a room and have a serious heart to heart with the ghost. Explain that the cleansing was a mistake and that there was a misunderstanding. Tell the ghost that there will not be any more cleansing rituals and that it is the wish of everyone involved to live peacefully. There is a very good possibility that apologizing to the ghost will set things back to how they were before the cleansing ritual. Talking to a ghost in this manner sounds crazy to the average person on the street, but the average person is not living with an out of control ghost!

Many families that have made this same cleansing mistake claim that talking to the ghost helped more than any ritual. However, do not make communicating with ghosts a regular event. Ghosts are the souls of the dead and should be kept at a distance. A normal ghost is not out to make enemies with the living. If talking to the ghost does not help, you can always move.

Q: I think my house is haunted, but I have not seen a ghost. How can I tell if my house is haunted?
A: Actually seeing a real ghost is a very rare occurrence. Most haunted houses exhibit the classic haunting characteristics (moving objects, strange lights, unidentifiable noises, unexplained footsteps, electrical interferences, doors that open and close by themselves, etc.). Using simple ghost hunting techniques such as taking photographs, videotaping, and using EVP audio recordings are good methods. Keep a journal of every event that seems to be ghost related. Eliminate all logical and natural possibilities. There does not have be apparition appearances for a house to be haunted.

Q: My husband and I live in a haunted house. We have both experienced the ghost. We have been in rooms where furniture has moved right before our eyes and yet my husband still refuses to believe that there are ghosts. What can I do to convince him that ghosts exist?
A: If a person is seeing furniture move and experiencing ghostly activity yet still does not believe in the existence of ghosts, there is nothing that can be done to persuade them otherwise. It is more comfortable for some people to not believe in the supernatural. Believing in ghosts shakes the very foundations of normal reality. If ghosts exist then every aspect of life is suddenly different. There are many people who come face to face with real ghosts only to later talk themselves out of the experience by explaining away the ghost sighting as a stress induced hallucination.

Q: Should I try to contact the ghost that lives in my home with an Ouija Board or should I bring in a psychic?
A: No and no. If communicating with a ghost is an absolute necessity, there is no need for an Ouija Board or a psychic. Simply talk to the ghost like a regular person. Many types of common ghosts can hear and understand the living. They are aware of what is going on inside the house and they can react to what people are saying. Communication should only be attempted when there is an absolute need; for example, when homeowners want a ghost to stop haunting

their child's room or they want the ghost to stop moving important files. A person should not talk to a ghost because they want a conversation or because they want to befriend the ghost.

Q: How can I tell the difference between a poltergeist and a ghost?
A: There are several things that make a poltergeist different from a ghost. Ghosts are souls of deceased people or animals while poltergeists may not be tied to any ghosts. It is believed that poltergeists are a form of psychokinetic (PK) energy controlled by an unknown human being. Ghosts appear without warning while poltergeists usually begin after a person's trauma. Ghosts are usually not malicious in nature, but poltergeists can become dangerous. A poltergeist will advance in stages. In the early stages of a poltergeist, it will be impossible to determine the difference between a poltergeist and a haunting. As the poltergeist progresses in levels, it will become clear that it is not a ghost.

Q: If electronic voice phenomena (EVP) recordings are possible then why haven't people been using this technique for years?
A: It is a misconception that EVP is a new phenomenon. EVP recordings have become very popular in the past decade with the ease and clarity of digital audio recorders, but the phenomenon itself dates back over one hundred years. Thomas Edison was one of the first to try to build a machine to communicate with ghosts. In October of 1920, an article appeared in American Magazine entitled, "Edison Working to Communicate with the Next World." This article confirmed that Edison was working on a secret project the goal of which was to communicate with the dead. Edison explained to Scientific American, "I don't claim anything because I don't know anything…for that matter, no human being knows. But, I do claim that it is possible to construct an apparatus which will be so delicate that if there are personalities in another existence who wish to get in touch with us…this apparatus will at least give them a better opportunity."

On June 12th, 1959, Friedrich Jurgenson, considered the father of EVP recordings, was recording bird songs when he noticed that there were unexplainable voices recorded on the tapes. At first,

Friedrich believed that he was picking up radio signals. He was intrigued by the voices and continued taping inside his house using microphones. His controlled experiments continued to produce results and he recorded more strange voices, some of which even called him by name and commented on his work. Jurgenson's hard work continued for another twenty-eight years until his death in 1987. He was convinced that the voices originated from the deceased.

An interesting fact that is unknown to many Catholics and Christians is that the Vatican was one of the locations for early EVP recordings. Two of the earliest EVP investigators were Italian Catholic priests, Father Ernetti and Father Gemelli, who came upon the strange phenomena by chance while they were recording Gregorian chants in 1952. The priests were deeply troubled by the paradox of recording ghost's voices and the Catholic teachings in regard to contacting the dead so the two priests visited Pope Pius XII in Rome. The Pope reassured them:

> Dear Father Gemelli, you really need not worry about this. The existence of this voice is strictly a scientific fact and has nothing to do with spiritualism. The recorder is totally objective. It receives and records only sound waves from wherever they come. This experiment may perhaps become the cornerstone for a building for scientific studies which will strengthen people's faith in a hereafter (Italian Journal Astra, June 1990 quoted Kubis and Macy, 1995:102).

The Vatican then gave permission for its own priests to conduct research into the ghostly voices. Father Leo Schmid, a Swiss theologist, collected more than ten thousand of them, which were published in his book When the Dead Speak in 1976, shortly after his death. Another Vatican approved researcher was Father Andreas Resch who conducted his own EVP experiments and began courses in parapsychology at the Vatican's school for priests in Rome.

Q: Can a ghost follow me home?
A: Ninety nine percent of the time the answer will be no, ghosts cannot follow a person home. However, there are a couple categories of ghosts that seem to be able to follow a person back to their home. The ghost usually follows the person because that person removed something of importance from the ghost's gravesite and the ghost wants the stolen item to be returned. When the item is returned or retribution has been repaid, the haunting will stop. It is a good idea not to take any items from a gravesite or from a haunted location. Of course, the haunting might be created by another supernatural entity such as a poltergeist. Poltergeists do not necessarily have anything to do with ghosts and they can freely travel to different locations.

Q: Can children see ghosts better then adults?
A: There is absolutely no evidence that children can see ghosts any easier than adults. This is actually a misconception originating from Hollywood movies and from the belief that a child's innocence gives them supernatural gifts. It is true that children are more likely to communicate with a ghost because they do not fully understand ghosts or the differences between life and death. Some types of ghosts who seek out communication with the living target children because they are more likely to openly communicate. Other than the greater likelihood to interact, children do not see ghosts that grown adults cannot experience.

Q: An old friend recently passed away and I was wondering if I could communicate with them again. Should I conduct a séance?
A: Séances will not work so do not bother trying them. It is also a belief that séances can attract negative energy and evil spirits. There is almost nothing that can be done to communicate with a deceased friend or loved one. If a person wants to express their feelings or say a final goodbye to a recently deceased friend then they should go to their gravesite and speak their mind honestly. It is a good release of grief and there is always a possibility that the deceased will hear them. Ghosts can communicate, but not everyone who dies will become a ghost. Ghosts are extremely rare. A person should not wish for their friend or loved one to become a ghost because common ghosts are typically very sad and live in their own pain and misery.

Q: The previous owner of my home committed suicide in the house. I constantly have dreams where I commit suicide. Is this man's ghost affecting my dreams?
A: There is a belief that a ghost can affect the dreams of the living however, in this case, it is possible that the bad dreams are purely a psychological effect of living in a house where a known suicide took place. If multiple people are having the same dreams then it is probably because of a ghost or energy left behind from the event inside the house. If only one person is having the dreams then it is probably a psychological effect. Try sleeping in different rooms throughout the house and changing sleep patterns. If, for any reason, the feelings about suicide creep into everyday life, seek out professional help right away from a licensed medical physician.

Q: I believe that my house is haunted. My dog will jump up and growl at nothing or slink out of the room. Is my dog sensing the presence of a ghost?
A: Animals can detect the presence of ghosts. Household pets will growl, bark, and even seem to attack unseen forces. The senses of animals are more acute and sensitive than the average human being. It has been documented that animals can detect and react to small changes in the natural environment. Animals know when earthquakes, thunderstorms, and natural disasters are about to take place because they can feel the small changes in the earth's electromagnetic fields. Animals use these same sense techniques to feel the presence of ghosts. When ghosts are present, the environment changes. The air ions change, the natural EMF's change, the temperature changes, etc. Household pets feel these environmental changes and react to them.

Q: I am positive that my house is haunted. My family is deeply religious. They do not believe in ghosts, but they do believe in demons. Several church approved groups have come to my house to get rid of the ghost, but all attempts have failed miserably. Now my church and my family are blaming me for this ghost. They are saying that my sins have invited this demon into the house and that I am the reason that it will not leave. Is any of this true?

A: No, none of this is true. The attempts failed to get rid of the ghost because nothing can remove a ghost. Most of the information from this family is based on common misconceptions and misinterpretations or faulty religious beliefs. It is a shame that a family would choose to condemn one of their own instead of admitting that there are things happening in the world that neither science nor religion can currently explain.

There are many religious orders that refuse to believe in ghosts despite the evidence, but ghosts continue to exist even when religions bury their heads in the sand. Christian beliefs dismiss ghosts because of the Bible interpretation that a person's soul goes straight to either Heaven or Hell at the moment of death with nothing in between. They believe this because the Bible does not mention an in between existence. However, it should be noted that there are sections in the Bible that do mention ghosts. In the Bible, King Saul consults with the Witch of Endor who makes the “ghost” of Samuel appear. The Bible makes it perfectly clear that there is a very active spirit world.

It should also be pointed out that an earlier religious belief was that the earth was the center of the universe and the sun, stars, and other planets rotated around the earth. Thousands of people were put to death for attempting to change that false belief with the truth. It is very hard to ignore the existence of ghosts without looking ignorant and arrogant. Religious change happens slowly and when faced with overwhelming evidence, religious leaders begin to rethink scriptural interpretations. The Reverend Monsignor, Professor C. Pfleger writes, “The facts have made us realize that between death and resurrection, there is another realm of post-mortal existence. Christian theology has little to say about this realm.”

Q: Should I bring in a psychic to get rid of the ghost haunting my house?
A: The theory that a ghost can be removed from its haunt comes up all the time. If there were a valid method to remove ghosts then there would not be any ghosts because someone would just eliminate them. Being a psychic has nothing to be with being able to force a ghost to

leave a house. The best psychic in the world has absolutely no control over any ghost. Psychics cannot control or direct ghosts to do anything that the ghost does not want or cannot do. Many of these cases tend to backfire on the homeowners. The psychic will try to cleanse the house of the ghost and instead of getting rid of the ghost; the paranormal activity will increase to an amount that makes it very hard to live with. Psychics are not the answer for getting rid of an unwanted ghost.

Q: Are ghosts more active on days when there are full moons?
A: There are theories that suggest that the moons electromagnetic pulls influence the activities of ghosts. The lunar gravity pull affects ocean tides. Animal studies show that physical activity, metabolism, aggression, and sexual behavior are dramatically increased in many species at the new and full moon. Both the moon and sun have numerous effects on the earth. It is believed that these effects help fuel the activity of ghosts. Ghosts are believed to increase their appearance and actions during full and new moon periods and when solar flares from the sun are hitting the earth.

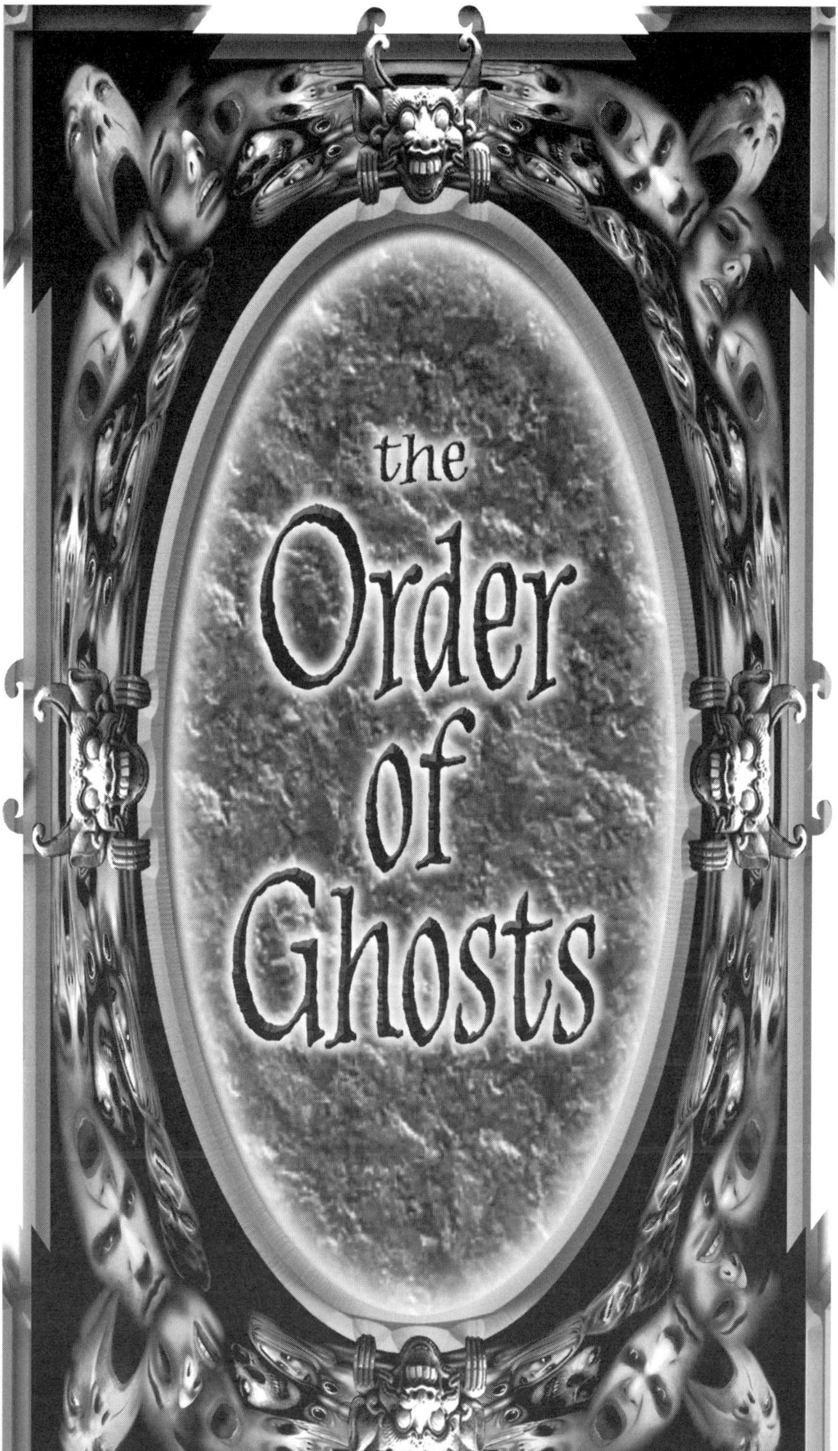
the
Order
of
Ghosts

The Difference Between Common and Malicious Ghosts

Common ghosts are the average ghosts that inhabit the world. These ghosts represent about ninety eight percent of all ghost sightings. Common ghosts are not malicious by nature. They are stuck on earth because of emotional ties that bind them here on earth. These ghost categories can overlap each other, meaning that some ghosts may fit into two or more categories. This system is designed to study the different personalities of ghosts. Paranormal researchers can begin to understand the complex nature of ghosts by studying their personalities.

Malicious ghosts represent about two percent of all ghost sightings. There is a huge difference between common ghosts and malicious ghosts. Malicious ghosts are basically parasites. These ghosts leach off of the living and drain life. They use fear to gain power and control over their victims. These ghosts cannot be trusted and should be considered hostile.

Although Poltergeists and Destroyers are not ghosts, but they are listed in this book because they are often confused as ghosts. Some people argue that they actually are ghosts. Leaving them out would be a mistake because these are entities that people will encounter and refer to as ghosts.

Ghosts know what lies beyond the land of the living. Studying ghost's personalities can help enlighten us into the secrets of the paranormal world. Discovering how and why ghosts are different is vital to uncovering their mysteries.

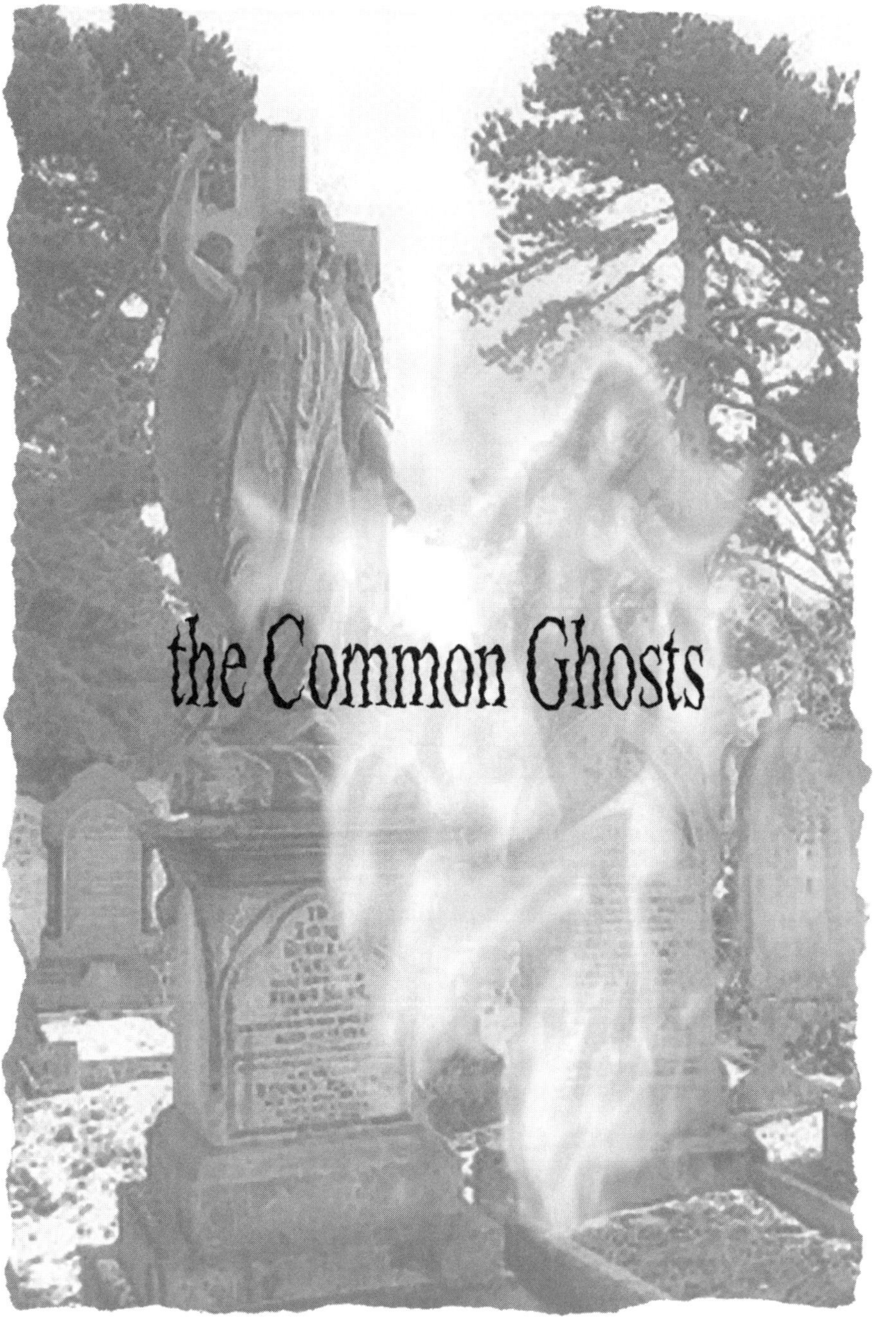
the Common Ghosts

the
Forgotten Child

The Forgotten Child

The forgotten child ghost is definitely the saddest of all ghosts. These ghosts are unwanted children, abandoned children, and abused children. They are the children that society has failed. These ghosts can be seen playing games alone or heard giggling and laughing in the dark. Even with all the misery they experienced in life, the ghosts of children act like children. They are playful, mischievous, and curious. They probably cannot understand or comprehend what has happened to them. These children were alone and lost in life and now are alone and lost in death. Their ghosts seek out love and attention. They are searching for the caring and protection that they never received in life.

Many of the oldest cases of forgotten child ghosts come from old closed orphanages where hundreds of unwanted children where packed together often abused by the people who were assigned to care for them. They were left in unclean and contaminated rooms where they developed sickness and disease. These poor children never experienced a normal childhood. They never played with toys and never knew the joy of a real childhood. They were unwanted and abandoned.

The sorrow of children is not something of the past. Today children continue to suffer alone in filthy inhumane conditions all over the world. Children die horrible deaths in hospital rooms where they are connected to machines pumping medications into their bodies to help ease the pain. No child should be left alone to die. In a perfect world, no child would be frightened, sick and suffering, abused and abandoned, but this is not a perfect world. It is a world full of pain. It is a world covered in the ghosts of children.

Jason Ross had lived much of his early life never thinking about ghosts or the paranormal until his twin daughters Julie and Sara started getting into ghost hunting as a hobby. Jason thought that it was a strange hobby for his young daughters, but at the time, he didn't believe in ghosts and thought it would be a good opportunity to spend more time with them. Julie and Sara became interested in ghost hunting while doing a report on the subject at their junior high school. They had made lists of all the haunted places around the area. Their dad would drive them and their friends to the locations.

One of the locations that the girls had heard about was the old Gore Orphanage in Lorain County, Ohio, not too far from Lake Erie. The rumor was that the orphanage had burned down with the children inside. The story was wrong, but at one time, there was a mansion and an orphanage on the grounds. The buildings dated back to the mid 1800's. The mansion was sold to a man who conducted occult rituals. He had two children that died in a diphtheria epidemic in 1893. It is believed that the children are still buried on the property in graves that are no longer managed by a caretaker. The ghosts of these children could be the source of the Gore Orphanage haunting.

Jason, his two daughters, and two of their friends arrived on the site after driving around searching for the location. (It is very difficult to find the exact location because the buildings are gone.) They wasted hours searching for the location and it was getting late, but they finally managed to find the four-foot stone pillar that marks the entrance to the grounds. The surrounding area is overgrown fields and forest with spotted remains of the old buildings. From the moment that the group entered the area, they felt as if someone was watching them. It was an eerie feeling that gave Jason, a forty-seven year old military veteran, goose bumps. Jason felt that the place was very creepy and he had a weird feeling in his gut. He shrugged the feelings off, attributing them to a lot of time spent driving and being in a strange place. Even as the group walked around taking pictures and shooting video, the sun was beginning to set and the shadows were growing long. The wind had picked up a little bit. The large tree branches above them began to strike together creating a loud creaking noise.

Julie, Sara, and their two friends were walking around taking photographs and joking about things to keep from becoming afraid when their equipment started to malfunction. The cameras stopped working and the video equipment started to show low battery, even though both cameras and camcorders were fully charged with new batteries before they left. Jason tried to keep his head with his children around, but for a split second he thought that he heard the giggling of a child. Only moments later, he heard the giggling again. One of his daughter's friends spoke up that he heard the giggling also.

As Jason walked over to one of his daughters to check the camera she was using, he felt something ice cold move past him. Jason said that the cold was like standing in front of a freezer with the door open. While it was late evening, this was still a hot summer day in Ohio and the temperature was still in the mid 80's. Seconds later, they all heard a child laugh. The ghost seemed to want to play with the visitors, but Jason felt that they had spent enough time ghost hunting. It was getting late and the group did not put up any fight to leave.

As the group started back to the car, the bushes off to the side of them started moving as if something was walking along with them. Back at the car, all of the equipment started working again and the girls were able to take more pictures. Later, after the photos were developed, the pictures taken at the orphanage property showed strange streaks of light and ghostly orbs. There was one strange picture that showed a tiny ball of light that looked much like a child's face peeking out of the bushes.

Jason does not go ghost hunting anymore and his daughters are now old enough to drive themselves to their ghost hunts. They believe that they photographed the ghosts of the old Gore Orphanage.

WHY DID YOU LEAVE ME?
the Angry Lover

The Angry Lover

The angry lover is the ghost of a jilted lover or spouse. These ghosts are more often male ghosts. They find out their partner is cheating on them or getting ready to leave the relationship. They are bitter, angry and jealous. They want revenge. They want to make their partner feel as bad as they as feel. The situation can end in violence with one or both lovers dead. Murder suicides are a common source for these ghosts. However, murder does not always have to accompany this ghost. Suicides are very common with the bitter lover ghost. Suicide is a way to force their lover to feel pain and responsibility for ending the relationship.

The angry lover ghost is a case of love gone horribly wrong. For them, love had become about control and obsession. There is no trust and no true affectionate emotions. It's not easy to accept that a partner is in love with someone else or has decided to end a relationship. The bitter lover ghost is filled with personal and emotional inadequacies. They could not handle an adult relationship with a partner who had equal control. Now, they cannot handle their loss of control. They often fall into the jealous false love "if I can't have them then no one can" syndrome. For these ghosts, their actions in life and death are all about retaking control. They are overcome with bitter anger and deep seeded fears, which usually leads down a path of violence and personal destruction.

As with most actions done in a moment of uncontrolled rage, the actions are later regretted. These ghosts are not evil, even if they committed a murder in life. They are confused and lost, just like many other ghosts. They seem genuinely sorry for their actions and are seeking ways to amend their earthly deeds. These ghosts will not be able to find forgiveness or punishment on earth, but they try to amend for their earthly deeds in the afterlife. They need to let go of life and the mistakes they made, but letting go has never been something that these souls were good at.

The Story of a Angry Lover

There is a cemetery in Carey, Ohio, with a strange history. The strange circumstances revolve around the tombstone for a husband and wife. Years before, the wife was found dead. She had been strangled to death, but no murder charges were ever brought because of the lack of evidence. The woman was buried in the cemetery and the husband went on with his life. Several years later, the husband passed away and was laid to rest in the plot next to his wife where they shared one large marble tombstone. Soon afterwards, an odd moss began appearing on the tombstone.

The tombstone was near the parking lot. Visitors started noticing that the unnatural lines from the moss were starting to form a picture on the tombstone. The scene forming on the marble tombstone was of the husband and wife facing each other with the husband's hands wrapped tightly around the wife's throat. Visitors with no prior knowledge of the tragic circumstances of the wife's death could accurately describe the horrible picture unfolding on the tombstone.

Word spread that the tombstone was depicting the true fate that had befallen the poor woman. The site attracted too much attention so cemetery officials had the tombstone replaced with a brand new tombstone. After some time passed, the exact murder scene reappeared on the new tombstone. The tombstone was cleaned many times, but the murder scene would just reappear strengthening the legend. The cemetery parking lot had become a huge attraction so the cemetery erected a wall in front of the tombstone to block its view from the parking lot. Many visitors who have seen the tombstone believe that it is the way for the murdered woman to reach out and express her unhappiness about her murderer being buried next to her.

the
Wounded Warrior

The Wounded Warrior

The wounded warrior is the ghost of a military soldier that has died as a result of fatal injuries received in military combat. They are common ghosts and will most often appear on old battlefields. Almost every battlefield on earth has wounded warrior ghosts. They can be seen dressed in military uniforms charging wildly into battle with their weapons held high, commanding people to get off the battlefield, or stumbling around injured in blood soaked bandages. Strange war related sounds and images are very common on haunted battlefields. Unsuspecting visitors report hearing gunshots and weapons clashing together while men scream and moan. The amount of ghosts can range from a single phantom to an entire army of ghosts. Phantom war scenes can be a traumatic sight to view.

Millions of soldiers fight and die for their countries. Whether the soldiers were from the World War II or from the Ancient Roman Empires, soldiers have always served their cause with honor and bravery, willing to go into Hell and give up their lives. Only combat veterans can truly understand the sacrifices, fears, and valor involved in combat. Duty and honor are more than words that a soldier speaks. They are sacred commandments. Men who march into battle together do so knowing that they might not return. A soldier's emotions become overpowering. Crippling injuries, the loss of limbs, starvation, inhumane front line conditions, madness, and death awaits soldiers on the battlefield.

The saying “war is hell” is precise. Combat conditions are nightmarish. Soldiers fight heroically while their enemy attempts to kill them. The fear builds and the powerful stress builds up on a soldier pushing them to emotional illnesses that they will live with forever. Watching friends die brutal deaths leaves gruesome images that get inside a soldiers mind haunting them for the rest of their life.

When a soldier falls in combat, there is a chance that their ghost will stand back up and continue the fight. The soldier refuses to let go of life and continues to fight the battle until they can find it in themselves to let go of the misery. To some soldiers, losing is not an option and death is not acceptable so they will continue to fight for their cause and continue to reenact the insanity of war forever.

The Story of a Wounded Warrior

World War II ended in 1945, but now, many decades after the close of that bloody war, witnesses are still seeing ghost planes over the Howden Moors of England. Visitors and locals can hear the whirling propeller driven airplanes and the rumbling of the massive bombers passing overhead when there are no planes visible in the clear skies. Other witnesses experience something much more disturbing; the visions of a massive B29 Superfortress going down and crashing into the Moors.

Like countless others before them, these witnesses desperately scramble to telephone local authorities. The local authorities have become so used to the reports that they know exactly what the witnesses are going to describe even before they get the chance. Witnesses hear the plane's engines spit and sputter under the distress of failure. The massive bomber appears to be losing control and descending fast into the Moors. The aircraft goes down behind the hills and crashes, exploding violently. The witnesses can hear the explosion and the grinding metal being torn to pieces from the force of the tremendous impact. The shocked witnesses can see thick smoke and sometimes the glow of fire rolling over the Moors. The sight is dramatic and powerful enough to traumatize.

The first sighting of the bomber crashing into the Moors brought out over one hundred volunteers and police officers to search for survivors. No plane debris or any other evidence of a horrible crash was discovered. Ghost planes have been seen by former pilots, which lend more credibility to the sightings not being a case of mistaken identity. Former pilots know planes and they know when they have seen a World War II Superfortress crash.

A local resident saw the massive bomber as its enormous shadow passed. He looked up to see the plane blotting out the sun. It continued for a moment before starting to shimmer and shake uncontrollably while dropping out of the sky. The plane dove from the sky and crashed somewhere in the gloomy Moors with an intense explosion. The local man knew right away that he had just seen the ghost of the B29 Superfortress.

These types of sightings had become so common that a local farmer decided to start a group to study the ghost plane sightings. When there is a sighting or when someone experiences something out of the ordinary, the farmer documents the information. Another local farmer had a strange experience when he hauled in a piece of aircraft wreckage, which litters the Moors, from his field to store it in his barn. He kept it stowed there until one night when his son saw the barn shake itself to pieces. The wreckage was returned to the field and no more incidents have happened since. Another witness recovered a World War II crewman's ring, which he said was given to him by the ghost of an airman in the Moors.

Locals believe that the Moors are the key to the ghosts that inhabit the area. Many of the ghost plane sightings occur near Sheffield, an area that was home to RAF and USAAF bases during World War II. The planes that went down in the Moors and killed their crewmembers were crippled in valiant dogfight combat by Germany's Luftwaffe fighter squadrons. The crippled aircrafts fell short of making it safely back to their bases and crashed violently into the murky Moors. Two of the numerous crashed planes were B29 bombers, which crashed in the same location killing their crews at the end of the war. All together, over fifty planes crashed into the Moors and over three hundred airmen lost their lives as a result.

Many paranormal researchers believe these ghost sightings are authentic because of the very similar detailed descriptions made by numerous unrelated witnesses. The Great War may have ended in 1945, but the young men who perished in the Moors are not ready to let it end.

the
Doomed Vessel

The Doomed Vessel

The doomed vessel is a phantom ship that haunts the high seas. These phantom ships were destroyed in tragedy on the treacherous oceans and are doomed to endlessly haunt the unforgiving seas. Typically, the ships sank in violent storms, smashed against sharp rocks in the dense fog, were attacked by pirates, or were destroyed in naval warfare. The crewmembers of these ships died awful deaths far from their homes. These sailors are terrible victims of unforgiving destiny.

Doomed vessels materialize out of nowhere in the middle of the ocean or in dense patches of fog. They can sometimes be seen flying over the water with sails full of phantom wind. These phantom vessels are perceived as death omens to other sailors. If sailors see a ghost ship, it means that something terrible is about to happen to their own vessel. There have been occurrences where sailors were able to actually board these ghostly ships and see that their operating systems were in tact and working properly despite no visible crewmembers at the controls. The phantom ships are always lost when unexpected storms roll in leaving the sailors to fiercely fight for the safety of their own ship.

Man has always been drawn to the sea. Drawn to the call of adventure and the passion to explore the unknown. But a sailor's life is hard work. Sailors navigate out into cold waters traveling far beyond the safety of land. They venture out to explore unknown lands or conquer enemy's abroad. To the sailors who lived most of their lives at sea, the vessels they sailed in were more than just sea vehicles. The vessels were homes to their crew and captain. Courageous sailors traveled out onto the unforgiving seas seeking adventure and glory, but sometimes, sudden tragedy was all that the sailors would find.

The ships themselves are only vessels made of wooden planks, steel bolts, strong ropes, and massive sails. The well-built ships were enormous and sturdy looking, but their size gave sailors a false sense of security. No ship, regardless of its size, is invulnerable. Tragedy goes hand in hand with sea travel. Giant waves roll up like monstrous walls crushing everything in their path. Even the strongest galleons did not stand a chance against the ultimate fury of Mother Nature. Crewmembers that went down with the ship were often the lucky sailors. After disasters, surviving sailors were left treading water in rough seas and shark-infested waters, slowly going mad from the baking sun and lack of fresh drinking water. Valiant sailors would fight passionately to save their ship from disaster. It was such a dishonor to abandon a sinking vessel that many captains would opt to go down with their ship instead of fleeing with the rest of their men.

The doomed vessels return to sail the seas once again. It is not known whether a single ghost is at the controls of this manifestation or if there are multiple ghosts working together to keep their vessel haunting the seas. Phantom vessels are some of the most eerie ghosts in the world. These ghosts echo the power of mankind's ability to build great wonders and the weakness of man as a mortal. These ghostly ships represent the fears of mankind. There is not a spot on earth that doesn't have a ghost story to share. Not even the beautiful oceans.

The Story of a Doomed Vessel

In April 1912, the “unsinkable” R.M.S. Titanic struck an iceberg and immortalized itself into the pages of history. One thousand five hundred thirteen people died horrible deaths as the enormous vessel sank slowly into the icy ocean. Even though the Titanic was lost deep at the bottom of the ocean, years later, a fisherman came forward saying that he had seen the ghost of the Titanic sailing toward the port where it should have arrived.

Just over twenty years ago, Jeff Norman was working on a fishing boat in the early morning hours of April. The air was filled with a strange fog. It seemed odd because of the way it moved. The fog seemed to dip and weave around as if it were alive. The waters were calm and there were no other ships in the nearby area. A few of the men were standing on the deck talking and repairing some fishing equipment when Jeff saw something out of the corner of his eye. Jeff thought it was the fog moving or just his eyes playing tricks on him, but he caught a glimpse of something again so he took a closer look.

At first there was nothing, but then the fog turned and whipped around clearing the view of the port side of a huge ocean liner not more than one hundred feet away. Jeff was in utter shock and he stumbled backwards at the sight. Before he could yell out, another fisherman yelled out that a ship was nearby. The fishing vessel sounded her foghorns and made a safety maneuver to keep from colliding or being hit hard by ocean waves. Jeff recalled that even at that time it was strange because there were no lights on the ship and there were absolutely no sounds coming from it. The water should have been churning from the large ship, but they were still. Jeff had never seen a vessel this size before. Even though he had just caught a glimpse of the ship, up close, dwarfing his own vessel, it was terrifying.

The fishermen stared intensely out into the fog searching for signs of the ocean liner. Their hearts were pounding with fear and panic. The fog twisted away for a moment, just long enough for the men to see the ocean liner one last time. This time, the men realized that something was terribly wrong. The ship appeared solid in some places, but in other places the ship seemed to be made of vapor. To their shock, the men also realized that the vessel was hovering several meters over the water as it drifted away silently.

The fog recovered the ship and the men did not see it again. Jeff became obsessed with his experience and began conducting his own research. He found out that the fishing ship he had been working on was in the path that the Titanic would have traveled if it had not hit the iceberg. Jeff said the other fishermen that were with him that morning would not talk about their experience. He needed to talk to people about this experience. As his research continued, he discovered that he was not alone in seeing the ghost ship Titanic. To his surprise, dozens of living people have reported similar run-ins with the phantom ship.

Even today, people are fascinated by the world's worst maritime disaster. There is a worldwide tour of artifacts from the Titanic. Almost from the beginning of the tour, the re-enactors reported strange occurrences revolving around the artifacts. Ghosts in period costumes appear and disappear in front of actors. Phantom footsteps and voices can be heard around the artifacts. A sad woman and a young child are the most common ghosts haunting the worldwide tour of Titanic artifacts.

the
Tormented Beast

The Tormented Beast

The tormented beast is a ghost animal. These ghosts were often abused and mistreated in life. They appear in varying spectral forms, just as other ghosts. They typically have bright glowing eyes, matted fur, strong claws, and sharp teeth. They sometimes have bloody, open wounds from injuries acquired in life. Animal ghosts are usually attached to a particular family or location. They can be seen as death omens when appearing to members of the same family. The family line is usually related to the onetime owners of the pet. Cats and dogs are the most common types of animal ghosts, but any animal can become a ghost, from family pets, to circus animals, and animals living in the wild.

Ghostly animals are usually, but not always, enraged with spite and fury. These animals will frighten away the living with scary shrieks, howls, and wild activity. Tortured animals eventually lose all trust in human beings and frenzy against anyone who comes in contact with them. These ghost animals often return from the grave angry and frustrated. They have high levels of aggression and are extremely territorial. They can attempt to bite, scratch, and attack to chase away human beings. They will chase away anyone who enters their territory unexpectedly. It's not that these animals are evil natured, but their brutal mistreatment has forced them to become untrusting rampaging victims.

Pain and misery is not exclusive to human ghosts. There are numerous types of phantom animals who were created out of torture and neglect. The murders of innocent animals often involve long and painful deaths. There are heartless people with no compassion that mistreat animals for no reason. There are also ghost animals created from legal and illegal animal experiments. Experimentation on animals can include painful surgeries involving tremendous agony and suffering. It's no surprise that some animal experiment laboratories are haunted with violent tempered ghosts.

Despicable animal torture is common around Halloween. Pet owners are often told to keep their pets indoors to avoid harm. Why people intentionally submit animals to cruelty and painful suffering is a mystery, but a warning must go out to them. One thing that ghosts teach the living is that what you do in life will have consequences that echo loudly in your afterlife.

The Story of a Tormented Beast

Volunteers at the lighthouse museum in Fairport Harbor, Ohio, tell tales of an eerie unexplainable nighttime visitor. In general, lighthouses seem to be common magnets for ghosts and paranormal activity, but the ghost who haunts this lighthouse walks on four legs. A black feline can be seen and heard running and playing throughout the lighthouse by visitors and volunteers. The cat has been seen out of the corner of volunteer's eyes, but it never could be caught or pinned in a room. No one could find or catch the wily feline, but it was constantly being seen and heard inside the lighthouse. The phantom cat became part of the lighthouse's folklore.

The volunteers in the museum said that they would hear the cat scampering around upstairs as if it was playing. The phantom cat never caused trouble besides the occasional fright from a sudden appearance. The curator who lived at the lighthouse claimed that the phantom cat would appear in their bedrooms at night and sit on the edge of their bed. The phantom cat was invisible but the curator could feel the weight of the cat pushing down on their covers. People often wondered what the story was behind the phantom cat. History shows that the previous owners wife had kept several cats in the lighthouse.

Skeptics always dismissed the ghostly cat as the figment of the workers imagination or said that a real cat had snuck into the lighthouse. However, in 2000, workers installing new air conditioning vents made a grisly discovery. The workers found mummified remains of a cat that had been trapped in the crawl space and preserved in the cold basement. The mummified cat's remains are now kept in a cardboard box at the museum. It has become a favorite attraction for schoolchildren touring the museum.

the
Broken Heart

The Broken Heart

The broken heart ghost clings to the earthly pain of losing a loved one long after death. They are suffering and isolated, searching endlessly for the true love that was lost to them. A majority of these ghosts are female. They are waiting alone and desperately searching for the soul of a dead child or waiting the return of their true love. They can be heard weeping sadly and singing gloomy songs. They can be seen gliding through beautiful fields or standing on the edge of a dangerous cliff. These apparitions are often a gray shade with long flowing hair, powerful eyes, and sometimes wear a cloak.

Death leaves us alone grieving in tormenting misery. For some people the loss of a loved one can be as devastating as their own death. For these unlucky souls no period of grief will be enough to cure the pain and suffering that they are feeling. Their heart desires closure, but instead, they are frustrated and guilt ridden. The broken heart ghost feels incredible heartache over the loss of their loved one. They are desperately seeking that love again so they can return to a happier time.

There is a saying that the moment a parent brings a child into the world is a moment that they become less selfish. A broken heart ghost can be a female searching for a lost child. The pain of losing a child is a private hell for a parent. Depression, sadness, and guilt can become a monster that devours all of life's energy. Parents can never cry enough tears for their lost children. Even in death, a mother can refuse to let go of that misery. The feelings of guilt have become so overwhelming that this ghost believes that it must suffer forever to make up for her child's fate.

Another broken heart ghost is the romantic female who waits patiently for the return of her true love. The ghost's true love might have been returning from battle or from a long overseas journey, but tragedy struck and fate decided that the man would never come home. During her life, the woman never gives up hope and pines away waiting for her lover to return. The days turn to months, months turn into years, and still no word of hope ever comes to this lonely spirit. The wait may seem pointless to others, but they do not know what true love means. For this passionate spirit, true love means keeping her promise to wait for her man to return home safely. The woman will wait until every ounce of life and sanity is drawn from her soul and after death comes, she will continue to wait.

The only thing that will help these ghosts is to be reunited with their lost loved one, but that is exactly what cannot be done as a ghost. Moving on after death takes a leap of faith. There must be a belief that after death loved ones will be united again. The grief, the misery, and the guilt must be forgotten. The broken heart ghost seeks to find their loved one here on earth, but the love of their life is waiting for them in the beyond.

The Story of a Broken Heart

In Albion Falls, Hamilton, Ontario, there is a legend that a young woman named Jane Riley threw herself from the falls after a failed love with Joseph Rousseau. The waterfall drop-off has since been nicknamed lovers leap. The locals grow up hearing different tales of the tragic legend.

Joseph's mother was quoted as saying, "let the blame rest on my shoulders," after Jane jumped to her death. Many years later, while still in good health, Joseph's mother was reported to have yelled out "Jane's hand is on my shoulder," just before she fell down dead.

The sad ghost of Jane Riley allegedly haunts the waterfall. One visitor to the falls said that he saw a woman in a strange looking dress jump from the top of the falls. He ran to the edge to look down, but he could not see anything from his position. As he moved close to the edge, he felt a cold hand on his shoulder. The man jumped and spun around, but there was no one there. He was alone. The man then, still confident that he had seen a young woman fall from the falls, ran down the side to find the girl. He reached the bottom expecting to find the young woman's mangled body crushed on the rocks, but there was no body. He searched around the area but could not find any evidence of the jumper.

To make the waterfall legends even worse, another young girl died at the falls in a terrible automobile accident when she lost control of her small truck, drove through a fence, and plunged over the falls.

the
Faceless Soul

The Faceless Soul

The faceless soul is a ghost that appears with a phantom body, but does not have a face. These ghosts have heads and hair, but no faces. The space appears black and hollow. They appear with other ghostly characteristics and act much like any other common ghost. Even though they do not have faces or eyes, these ghosts will turn their heads to look in a certain direction.

The missing face seems to symbolize a secret personal or physical imperfection. The missing face can symbolize embarrassment and shame. In some cases, the ghost had something awful happen to their face when they were alive. Now in death, they still seem unable to deal with their human disfigurement. These ghosts linger in regret and trauma left over from their past life. They are unable to escape the ghostly prisons, which they themselves have created.

Faceless soul ghosts can be a very terrifying sight for witnesses. The only thing scarier then a ghost with a monstrous face is a ghost with no face. They have no voice and do not make any sounds. They can be seen floating silently above the floor or gliding through rooms.

Human beings are very visual. First impressions are important and people make snap judgments based on appearance. There is a psychological effect of going through life with a disfiguring facial scar or a personal secret. These ghosts carry that burden into the afterlife. The same first impression snap judgments can be said about the living who run into these faceless ghosts. Many people see these faceless ghosts as evil or monstrous even though they have never done anything to cause harm.

Faceless soul ghosts lack identity. It is hard to track down the real identity of a ghost that does not have a face. These ghosts feel as if they were unknown or not worthy of being recognized in life so they will continue to be anonymous in death.

The Story of a Faceless Soul

Scott from Indiana has a problem with his house. A mysterious, faceless ghost haunts it. Scott and his wife have lived in the house for five years. Scott's wife and other friends and family members have seen the faceless specter on several occasions, but Scott has never seen it. On one occasion, Scott's younger brother was visiting from Florida. He was sleeping in the guest bedroom when he was awoken by the sound of items being moved on the dresser. As his eyes focused in the darkness, he could see the back of a woman facing the dresser. She had long flowing hair and was wearing a white nightgown.

At first, he thought it was Scott's wife getting something from the dresser, but the body type and hair were wrong. Scott's brother said, "Hello." The woman stopped moving items on the dresser. There was a brief moment of silence and tension. Scott's brother contemplated that this could be a robber or someone else who had snuck into the house. His thoughts soon changed as the woman slowly rose up off the floor and started to rotate in midair. The ghost hovered above the floor and turned to face the bed.

Scott's brother got his first look at the faceless ghost. There was only blackness where the face should have been. He sat up quickly and started to yell and scream at the top of his lungs. The ghost instantly vanished before his eyes. He jumped out of bed and darted from the room. Bolting into the hallway, he almost collided with Scott and his wife who had come to see what the screaming was about.

After explaining the situation, Scott's brother packed up his clothes and went to a hotel. He vowed never to return to the house again. Two years have passed and he has never stepped foot back inside the house.

Scott had always thought of the ghost stories as a bad joke. He had lived there five years listening to them, but never saw the ghost until recently. Scott was injured while putting up some drywall when a board slipped and hit him in the face. The cut was pretty deep. He went to the hospital and received dozens of stitches.

When Scott came home from the hospital, he laid on the couch while his wife took care of him. She needed to go to the store to pick up some medication for him. Scott was half asleep on the couch when he felt an icy cold touch on his face. The touch was so cold that it was almost like an icy burn on his fresh wound. Scott slowly opened his eyes and, for the first time, saw the faceless ghost standing overtop of him with her arm down gently touching his wounded face. As Steve slowly sat up, the ghost backed away. The ghost put its hands overtop of the black cavity where its own face should have been and disappeared.

Scott has not seen the ghost since that day, but now he believes in its existence. He believes that the ghost must have had something happen to its own face when alive and was saddened to see that he had hurt his face in the accident.

the
Shadow Builder

The Shadow Builder

The shadow builder is a dark, mysterious, and intelligent phantom. Shadow builders manifest in the shadows of life. They are very intellectual and knowledgeable specters that can manipulate and control shadows. The best way to physically describe a shadow builder is a solid, walking shadow often reported to have glowing eyes. They are described as human-like in form, but still like a shadow that can flow illusively and quickly into dark corners. Their touch is icy cold like that of death.

People tend to first become aware a shadow builder's presence by seeing them out of the corner of their eye. Witnesses catch a quick glimpse of movement in the shadows. Most people who see them will put off their first sighting as an overactive imagination. The shadow builder's movements are fast and masked in the safety of the shadows. Real shadows give camouflage to this elusive phantom.

Shadow builders have their own agenda. Their needs and interests are kept secret. They see the world from a different viewpoint. Their supernatural knowledge gives them an advantage over the living. They can manage and influence the world around them to varying degrees. Shadow builders are very powerful and can be extremely intimidating. These phantoms could be working inside an unknown supernatural system or hierarchy of supernatural spirits. They are believed by some to communicate and work together with other phantoms.

Shadow builders are the enigma of ghosts. These ghosts are not tied down to a single location. They can be present anywhere at anytime. These phantoms decide whether or not they will communicate with people. They choose how they will communicate and what information they will provide. Shadow builders have been mistaken for angels, demons, time travelers, inter-dimensional beings, aliens, and even the grim reaper.

People who communicate with a shadow builder phantom will carry a strange friendship throughout their lifetime. At times, they may even come into contact with other shadow builders. Shadow builders can interact with the living and provide secret information about the past, present, and future. They know things that are seemingly unknowable because they are working on a higher supernatural level than other normal ghosts. They never offer the living access to all of their secrets and keep their real intentions hidden. Shadow builders offer a strange look into the shadowy world of ghosts.

The Story of a Shadow Builder

Thomas O'Connor thought that he must have been going crazy when he started seeing shadows moving and gliding around the basement of his home. His experiences started out very simple. During some spring-cleaning, Tom was emptying boxes in the basement. He kept seeing shadows moving out of the corner of his eye. When he would take a closer look, the shadows stopped moving. Nothing was there but dust and shadows. Tom finished the cleaning and went on with his life.

The phantom seemed to be most active in the basement. Tom still had not seen the phantom, but he had the feeling that something odd was happening in his house. Things remained quiet for a few months until Tom's wife ran up from the basement screaming hysterically. She said that she saw someone with red eyes staring at her in the basement.

Despite the weird moving shadows, Tom figured that the eyes were probably from a cat or wild animal that had gotten into the basement. He went down to investigate. He looked around the basement, but could not find anything. Then suddenly the shadows seemed to gather around themselves. In the middle of the shadows was a set of red glowing eyes peering back at Tom from the darkness.

Tom knew right away that these eyes were not from a wild animal. His heart was pounding and he was utterly terrified.

Not knowing what to do next and not knowing what this monster was going to do to him, Tom started to slowly back up toward the steps. Just then, the shadows shifted. They seemed to build on themselves forming a human-like shadow figure. It was strange, but suddenly Tom felt calm and more relaxed. Some of his fear seemed to be lifted away. Just when Tom thought that his experience could not get any stranger, the figure spoke to him in a human voice saying, "Hello Tom, do not be afraid of me." Tom was shocked, but he choked back his voice to ask, "What are you?" Its' reply was simple, "I am a friend." The phantom went on to say that it could help Tom and his family. Then it disappeared without warning.

Tom explained to his wife what had happened to him. He told her not to be afraid of this phantom, but she would not go back into the basement and wanted to sell the house. Tom continued going down into the basement every evening to wash clothes for the family and to have long conversations with the shadowy being. They talked about philosophy, history, religion, and current events. Tom never felt threatened by the phantom.

Tom and his wife were having some serious marital problems because of their new visitor. She desperately wanted him to stop communicating with the phantom. On one visit to the basement, the shadow builder lived up to its' promise to help Tom's family. It told Tom that his wife had breast cancer. Tom went straight upstairs and told his wife. Sure enough, an examination revealed a malignant tumor in one of her breasts. The information provided by the phantom caught the cancer in the early stages and helped saved the life of Tom's wife. Tom believed that the phantom's information helped his wife get quick treatment for the cancer, but his wife believed that the phantom knew about the cancer because it created the cancer. Tom's wife filed for divorce and moved out of the house. Tom was left alone with the phantom that he still claims to be in contact with to this day.

the
Awakened Sleeper

The Awakened Sleeper

The awakened sleeper is a ghost that was dormant, but has been awakened by the living. Awakenings tend to occur in very old buildings (homes, hotels, theaters, etc.) that are undergoing renovations. These hibernating ghosts can also be awakened by new construction on holy ground or spiritual points of worship. The construction workers are completely unaware that their restoration effort is going to awaken the fury of a sleeping ghost. There is often no previous record of a haunting. The location may have never experienced any kind of paranormal activity in the past because the ghost was content with its surroundings.

When renovations and construction begin, these once quiet ghosts suddenly become extremely active. An awakened sleeper ghost will start small by moving objects like construction tools or personal items. They will slowly take control of electrical power tools causing them to turn on and off without warning. The ghosts can make huge heavy objects fall over crashing down dangerously close to workers. They exploit this paranormal activity to let the living know that they are not happy about the current renovations. The ghosts are trying to warn the construction workers that they are not welcome. The type of paranormal activity created by these ghosts will start off small and simple. It will continue to escalate if the ghost's early warnings are not heeded.

These types of haunts are power struggles between the living and the ghost. The ghost will share its' property with the living, but it feels as if it is the sole owner of the property. It sees the living as visitors. The ghost feels that no one else has the right to make changes to its' property. The fatal flaw in the ghost's belief is that the ghost is dead and no longer owns anything. This world is for the living.

Regardless, awakened sleeper ghosts are very persistent and can be quite persuasive. They will use their supernatural powers to frighten away workers and create construction delays. They have even been blamed for destroying some construction locations by causing floods and fires. While some of these ghostly activities can be dangerous, these ghosts are not evil in nature. For the most part, an awakened sleeper ghosts does not want to harm people. They are very territorial and are trying to protect what they see as their home. How far the ghost will take the haunting depends on the personality of that ghost. Some ghosts may be content with frightening workers away from the site while never becoming violent. Other ghosts may feel it necessary to take the haunting a step further and cause problems that may harm an unsuspecting worker. Awakened sleeper ghosts have also been blamed for accidentally causing heart attacks by frightening older construction workers.

Once a sleeping ghost has been awakened, typically, a haunting will begin. In the early stages of these haunts, the ghost will single out a few workers to pick on continuously. When the workers finally decide to tell their other coworkers about their paranormal experiences, they are almost always met with playful ridicule. However, the haunting activity will soon increase to encompass the entire construction crew until it reaches a point where no worker feels comfortable working alone on the site. On more than a few occasions, large, masculine construction workers have walked or even ran off of job sites swearing to never return again all because of the unrelenting actions of a single ghost.

The Story of an Awakened Sleeper

Jay Lewis has been a construction worker in Seattle, Washington, for fifteen years. He has worked on hundreds of renovation projects. He never encountered anything out of the ordinary until he got a call to start renovating a downtown building. The building was over eighty years old. Jay's construction company was brought in to renovate three floors of the building.

The first two weeks of the renovation project went pretty smooth except for the occasional missing tool, which is not necessarily an abnormal thing. Tools are commonly lost and stolen from worksites. However, soon afterwards, the construction workers started hearing strange noises and voices that seemed to be coming out of empty rooms. Many of the workers dismissed the voices as natural building echoes, but there were a few workers who believed that something else was happening at this construction site. Some workers started complaining that they saw objects move without explanation. There were even reports of strange people being seen walking into rooms, but when a worker would chase them down, the room would be empty. The strange people could never be pinned in a room.

Jay had not seen anything out of the ordinary for himself until one early morning. He was on the site with a couple of other co-workers. The workers were frustrated because tools had been turning up missing the past couple of days. Telephones had been hooked up in every room, but the telephone service was not yet activated. All of a sudden, the telephones started to ring in different rooms at different times. The stunned workers tried answering a few of the telephones, but they were always dead.

Jay was carting some plywood down a hallway when the telephones finally stopped ringing. As Jay moved closer to the far end of the hallway, a woman stepped out of the last room and walked down the hallway. Jay was startled by the woman and told her that the area was off limits as she crossed the hallway. The woman turned as if she was going to enter another room. Instead, she walked right into the wall and passed through it vanishing in front of Jay.

These types of paranormal activity continued until the construction team was done with the renovations. By the end of the renovations period, workers were constantly looking over their shoulders and jumping at the slightest movement. Many of the workers had been frightened so badly that they would not go back into certain areas alone. The tension had become so serious that the workers were told not to play any practical jokes because the ghosts were keeping everyone on edge. Jay was more than happy to finish that job and move on to another site, but he will never forget what happened on that early morning. He does not know if the ghosts are still haunting the newly renovated building.

the
Searching Amputee

The Searching Amputee

The searching amputee ghost is a victim looking for their missing bodily limb. These ghosts are commonly sufferers of an automobile or train accident or soldiers who have experienced the tremendous carnage of war. Ghosts can hunt for missing arms, legs, and even a missing head. These ghosts are suffering with the traumatic event of seeing their own limb torn away from their body. Many times, it is the last thing that they experienced before death. Sometimes these ghosts are searching for limbs that were not buried with them for various reasons. They are reaching out for the absent pieces that would make them feel whole again.

Human bodies are such an important part of how people see themselves that losing a limb can be almost as devastating as death. When limbs are lost, amputees replace them with artificial prosthetics. Human beings need limbs for everyday life, but death frees the soul from constraints of the body. The body is only organic matter, a mass of cells and tissues, a container for the soul. The soul is all that truly matters, but some souls feel incomplete without all of their body. These ghosts need to recover their missing body parts before they can rest in peace. Once the missing limb is placed with the other remains, the ghost usually stops haunting. After the missing limb has been recovered, the ghost may reappear, but will manifest whole with its previous missing body part intact.

In some very strange cases, there are reports from other witnesses of limbs being seen floating in the air. Oddly enough, the limb seems to be searching for its missing body.

The searching amputee ghost is caught up in personal issues and obsessions that revolve around a missing piece of human flesh. They have died and are released from the limitations of the organic body, but in this great process, they are failing to realize some very important aspects of human existence. Human beings are more than flesh and blood and more than what can be seen in a mirror.

The Story of a Searching Amputee

The bloodiest day in U.S. military history happened during the American Civil War in Antietam, Maryland. General Robert E. Lee and the Confederate army marched into Antietam against numerically superior Northern forces. By nightfall, 26,000 men had fallen in battle. It was the bloodiest day of the entire war.

There was a vantage point on the battlefield at one time held by the Union soldiers. Union troops used the strategic location to fire on Confederate troops as they fell back down the road. One Union soldier said that killing the Confederates was as easy as shooting animals in a pen. The retreating Confederates were slaughtered and their bodies fell piling up to four and five high. The area became known as Bloody Lane.

Out of all the places on the Antietam battlefield, the Bloody Lane is the most haunted. Strange glowing lights, odd vapor mists, phantom gunshots, and apparitions have all been reported at this spot. Visitors often report hearing phantom war cries from the Irish Brigade units, which lost sixty percent of their force that day.

Stan Jennison, a Civil War fanatic, visited the Antietam battlefield one June afternoon. He had always been interested in the history of the Civil War, but had never thought about ghosts or the paranormal. Stan was causally walking up the Bloody Lane road taking in the scenery when a Union soldier stepped out from a group of trees off to his side. The soldier had his head down and seemed to be searching the ground for something. Stan thought that he was looking at an actor who might have dropped something on the ground so he started to walk over toward him to see if he could help. As the soldier turned, Stan saw that the soldier was missing an arm. The wound looked fresh. The side of his uniform seemed to be soaked in blood. The soldier stopped what he was doing and looked up at Stan.

It was a stare that chilled Stan to the bone and made all of the hairs on the back of his neck stand straight up. He knew that this was not an actor. The soldier started to fade away and then vanished.

Stan could not explain what he had just seen, but now, looking back on that day, he is grateful that this ghost appeared to him. Stan feels that this ghost gave him a lot into the hardship of the Civil War that reading books and studying battles could never give him. He feels that the soldier was probably searching for his lost arm. Thousands of Civil War soldiers lost limbs to cannon fire. The horrible American Civil War is long over, but the phantom drums still beat and the ghosts of the past still haunt the battlefields.

INFIRMARY
the
Horrific Vision

The Horrific Vision

The horrific vision ghost is the strange manifestation of an illusion of a real life past event. This very strange ghost sighting involves seeing a specific scene from the past. These visions are usually gruesome and terribly frightening. They can be horrible war, painful hospital or violent murder scenes, which are visually traum atic to witnesses. While these visions usually appear in full color with real life forms, they rarely manifest with any sounds. The visions are often eerily silent.

It is unknown whether these horrific visions are being produced from a single ghost or from the combination of several ghosts working together. The ghosts in this vision do not always acknowledge the presence of the living witnesses, but there are times when a single ghost from the vision will acknowledge the living with a causal glance, by mouthing words or through eye contact. This subtle form of communication is very important because it verifies that these types of visions are not part of a random projected playback.

These visions are what the ghosts experienced in life. They seem to need to express and share their experience with the living. It's almost as if these ghosts are seeking help and understanding from the living. Showing their situation through this horrific vision is their way of reaching out to the living. These ghosts are trapped in the past, locked forever in one moment of time. Witnesses are shocked and sometimes traumatized by these visions. The witnesses are frozen in fear watching these ghastly visions unfold before their own eyes. Those who forget the past are doomed to repeat the mistakes of the past. The horrific vision ghosts will never let the living forget the past.

The Story of a Horrific Vision

Wenona Whitefeather was visiting a location in Colorado marked as a national historic site with her husband when they saw a terrifying ghostly vision of the past. The couple was drawn to visit the location know as the Sand Creek Massacre because their ancestral lineage ties them to the Cheyenne Indians that once roamed that land. The site was peaceful and therapeutic, but as the couple walked

together over a small hill, the peacefulness of the scenery suddenly and drastically changed. Before their very eyes, the couple says, dozens of dead American Indian woman and children appeared scattered over the ground. They looked as if they had been murdered. The scene was brutal and bloody. Some of the dying American Indians were rolling around in agony. They looked like they were screaming, but there were not any sounds. The vision was graphically powerful beyond description. The site was so intense that Wenona buried her head in her husband's chest and started to cry. Her husband looked down at Wenona for only a split second, but when he looked back up, the vision was gone. The land was at peace again. It was a terrible reminder of the past and something that Wenona will live with for the rest of her life.

The land that Wenona and her husband visited is known as the Sand Creek Massacre site. At dawn on November 29, 1864, 700 U.S. volunteer soldiers attacked a village of about 500 Cheyenne and Arapaho Indians. The soldiers used small arms and howitzer fire to drive the Indians from their camp. Many managed to successfully flee from the attack, but many women, children, and elderly made the mistake of fleeing into the bottom of a dry streambed. The American soldiers followed and shot them as they struggled through the sand. Over the savage seven-hour attack, 150 Indians were slaughtered. During the following day, the soldiers wondered around the camp committing further atrocities on the dead bodies before leaving. Many years have passed, but the land has never forgotten the misery.

the
Mischievous Trickster

The Mischievous Trickster

The mischievous trickster is a ghost that enjoys playing harmless games with the living, such as moving personal objects or knocking on doors and windows to get attention. It is a playful ghost that doesn't mean any harm or malicious intent. These ghosts fool people, do outlandish things, and then disappear. They do not use their abilities to cause destruction, but as a way of getting noticed. They can manifest in many different forms just like other categories of ghosts and their characteristics will vary depending on the personality of the particular ghost. These ghosts are never violent or temperamental. They are driven by the reactions of the living to their games. They try to seek out people who are not afraid or bothered by their games. These ghosts like people with a curious nature who will play along with the games.

Moving objects is a common characteristic of all types of ghosts, but the trickster ghosts make a special habit of relocating items so that people will have trouble finding them quickly. These items could be common things like a set of car keys, earrings or maybe a letter. It is important to note same people are just plain forgetful or careless with personal items. A trickster ghost cannot be blamed for that. If someone is constantly missing items, it is probably just their careless nature. Nevertheless, when these trickster ghosts are present, people should expect the unexpected.

The mischievous trickster ghosts also have other bad habits that include knocking on doors and windows so that people have to go and see who is knocking. The ghosts will turn lights on and off and gently tap people on the shoulders. While most of this activity can be very frightening for people who have never dealt with ghosts before, it is actually a harmless game not meant to hurt or scare anyone. In many cases where people live with these types of ghosts, if they have children or feel afraid, they will ask the ghost to stop doing whatever is frightening them and the ghost will obey. Most accidents tend to happen when a person is shocked or frightened by the presence of a ghost and they run away hysterically, hurting themselves in the process.

The mischievous trickster ghost tends to be a very active ghost and will continuously play these types of hide and seek games, sometimes on a daily basis. It can become somewhat of an inconvenience for the people involved with this ghost. There is an important distinction between this ghost's playful activity and other ghosts who move items for the purpose of making the living believe that the items themselves are alive. Trickster ghosts do not move objects to give an impression that the objects are alive. They are not trying to give objects human-like characteristics. These ghosts do not want to directly control the living nor do they want to frighten or harm the living. The mischievous trickster ghost is a strange apparition. They can be caring, terrifying, and mischievous all at the same time.

The Story of a Mischievous Trickster

Sheri had always been close with her brother Jim. He was eight years older than her and when they were kids he liked to hide her toys and play childish tricks on her. Nothing mean, but the typical big brother nonsense. Jim was 32 years old when he died of cancer. He had been diagnosed only 8 months before. His death was an extremely hard blow to Sheri. He had spent the last few months in Sheri's guest room while she took care of him. She held his hand as he slipped away.

A few months after Jim's death, Sheri started noticing some strange events happening around her home. A book of old family pictures that Sheri had been looking at was opened and some pictures of Sheri and Jim together were taken out of the photo holders. Sheri did not remember taking the pictures out, but she decided to hang them on the refrigerator.

A couple days later, Sheri heard a loud crash upstairs. She went up to investigate the noise and found a box of Jim's personal stuff spilled all over the floor. There was a letter that had fallen out of the box with Sheri's name on it. She had not seen the letter when she was putting away Jim's affairs. Jim had written the letter to Sheri. It talked about all of the fun times that they had had together over the years. It also thanked her for being in his life and helping take care of him. The letter also mentioned that he was sorry for all the mischief that he did to her as a child. This brought back memories that made her smile. He jokingly added that if he had it to do all over again, he would.

More time passed and Sheri started to notice that small objects were disappearing from her house. She was bewildered. Sheri stood in the kitchen trying to think of where she could have left her personal items. As she was thinking, the picture of her and Jim slipped away from the refrigerator magnet and landed at her feet. As she picked up the picture, she started to think about Jim and how he would always take her toys and hide them under his bed when they were children.

Sheri thought that it was crazy, but she could not resist the feeling to look under the spare bed. Sure enough, in the spare bedroom where Jim had been staying, she found every lost item under the bed in a small pile. This scared Sheri. She didn't know what to think about this strange experience. Items continued to turn up missing and each time they were always found under the spare bed. Sheri isn't afraid anymore. She has never seen Jim or talked to him, but she can feel his presence and seems willing to put up with his practical jokes.

the
Lost Traveler

The Lost Traveler

The lost traveler is the ghost of someone who died suddenly or was murdered while traveling to a specific location. These ghosts are often very pale looking, have a cold pale appearance, and wear the same clothing from their last night on earth. They almost always look out of place and seem sad but friendly. They tend not to speak too much other than to tell people where they are traveling or ask questions about their current location. They sometimes talk about the weather and are inclined to keep all conversations very short.

The most common forms of these ghosts are phantom hitchhikers. Phantom hitchhikers are ghosts who stand at the edge of the roadway at night trying to flag down drivers to help them reach their final destination. These ghosts appear distraught on the route of their demise, sometimes in the exact spot of their death. They are either trying to get to the location they were going before their death or they are just trying to get home. After an unsuspecting person picks up the traveling ghost, the two travel together until the automobile passes a certain location (the place of the ghost's death, a graveyard, the ghost's home, or the ghost's final destination) where the ghost will then vanish before the very eyes of the surprised driver.

The lost traveler ghosts are reaching out for help from beyond the grave. They feel that they need the help of the living to reach their final destination. Maybe they seek the comfort of human companionship to help them through this grueling experience. These ghosts are lonely. From the ghost's perspective it is trying to complete that perfect night that was robbed from them by death. Their desires are never fulfilled because each time these ghosts reach their destination, just like some cruel joke, they are reset back at the place where they died and forced to try again to reach their destination. Being returned to the starting position over and over should be an important clue to these ghosts to stop trying, but it turns out to be just the opposite. The lost traveler ghost continues to work harder to reach their destination for the opportunity to relive that final night.

Various types of lost traveler ghosts can be found in the legends of almost every culture, some dating back thousands of years when these phantoms would appear to people on horse trails. These ghosts are all stuck in a cycle of a recurring nightmare. They are searching for a way to arrive at the safety of their home where their loved ones are surely awaiting their return. It is almost as if these ghosts are ignoring death to cling to the responsibilities of their life.

The lost traveler ghost wants to relive a night from their life that was taken away from them prematurely, but nothing that they do now will ever satisfy those horrible feelings of hopelessness and despair. These ghosts will never reach their final destination. Their time on earth is over and nothing can be done to recapture those precious lost moments of life. These ghosts are trying to complete a journey that has already ended.

The Story of a Lost Traveler

Andrew and his friend Aaron were driving around on a Friday night trying to waste some time until his girlfriend could get off work. They cruised the local back roads talking and listening to music. Andrew finally got a call from Holly, his girlfriend. She was on her way home. The guys were to meet her there in about twenty minutes.

Andrew came out of the back roads and onto the main route, which was still not a high traffic road. They were about seven miles from Holly's house. At one point in the road, there is a long straight stretch of road that has created many fatal auto accidents. Impatient drivers like to pass cars on that stretch even in fog and bad weather. Teens drag race up and down the road on the weekends.

In the middle of the straightaway, the guys saw a flash of light ahead of them on the road. The object was out of visual distance. Andrew slowed down. A few moments later, they passed a strange woman standing at the edge of the road. She was staring down the road. Andrew slowed the car more, but the woman did not look at the car or try to make eye contact with either of the two young men. The guys debated whether they should stop to see if she needed help, but decided to keep going. They did not see a wrecked car and she did not try to flag them down so they thought that she must not be having trouble despite being out there alone.

When the guys arrived at Holly's house to pick her up, they told her about the strange lady at the side of the road. Holly made jokes about being too chicken to stop the car. They decided to go back down the road to see if the woman was still out there alone.

As they drove closer to the location, they could see the woman still standing at the edge of the road. This time, Andrew pulled off the road. He put down his window and asked the woman if she needed any help. The woman finally looked down at him and answered, "I need a ride." Andrew asked where she was going, but she did not answer. He told the woman that they were going into town. The woman replied, "I will go to town."

Aaron was now sitting in the backseat so he opened up the door for her. The woman got inside the car and they started to drive toward town. The woman did not say anything even after the others introduced themselves. Andrew recalls how odd the woman acted, like she was in shock. He asked her if she was in an accident. That seemed to snap the woman out of her daydream state and she replied, "Yes, I was in an accident."

The group was shocked to hear that the woman was in an accident, but that did not explain her weirdness. They were about two miles from town when the woman asked them to stop. Andrew asked why and if there was something wrong. The woman just said, "There's trouble if I pass my home." Andrew slowed down a little, but he did not know what to do because there was no way that he was going to let this woman wonder around on the road at night in her condition. The woman pointed ahead and said, "Home." Ahead was the Woodland Park Cemetery.

Andrew stopped the car in front of the closed cemetery gates. While he was dialing his cell phone to call for help, Aaron and Holly looked over at the cemetery. When Andrew looked up into the rear view mirror, the woman was gone. "Where did she go?" He shouted.

Aaron and Holly immediately turned. The woman had vanished from the car. The car door had not opened, but she was gone. The three sat confused trying to figure out what to do next. They continued to drive into town and told their friends about the mysterious vanishing woman. Most of their friends thought they were making up the story as a joke. Some of them had driven up and down that road several times that night and never saw a woman standing on the edge of the road.

The cemetery where the woman disappeared is where many of the people who died in car accidents on that back road were buried. The three friends believe that this woman was a ghost of someone who died on that road and is buried in that cemetery. They are still investigating.

LIBRARY

the
Vengeful Wraith

The Vengeful Wraith

The vengeful wraith is a ghost that returns from the dead to avenge a misdeed perpetrated on them in life. The misdeed is usually the sin of murder. The wraith haunts and torments the perpetrator until they confess their crimes, go insane with grief or commit suicide. There is no escape from a wraith. It is obsessed with its' mission of revenge. It will never stop haunting the wrongdoer until its quest is completed.

Wraiths come in all shapes and sizes. They can be a murdered lover returning to avenge their death. They can be a past relative coming back to haunt someone who is causing trouble for their family. The ghost can also be haunting a person who stole an important possession from them, from a friend or from a loved one. Revenge ghosts are extremely rare apparitions.

Criminals believe that they can escape the long arm of the law and avoid punishment. They believe that they are smarter than the law and, in some rare cases, can escape earthly justice. While they may have escaped an earthly justice, they will never escape the supernatural justice that is waiting patiently for them. Wraiths can torment their murderers with visions of their crimes for the rest of their lives.

When a heartless person kills, they rob the victim of the most sacred gift of all - life. They take away the hopes, future dreams, and everything material from their victims. They take away family, friends, and loved ones. They leave behind a black hole of emptiness. It should not be a total surprise that some angry ghosts return after death seeking retribution for the crimes perpetrated against them in life. When the earthly laws have failed, criminals may think that they are getting away with their hideous crimes, but the vengeful wraith will always be there to carry out its' own special brand of supernatural justice.

Revenge ghosts are also associated with deathbed curses. When a dying person speaks a nasty curse on a person, it is believed that a revenge ghost will return to carry out the promise of that curse. The revenge ghost will continue to carry out the punishment of the curse until the person has made suitable atonement for their actions or until the cursed person is dead. Vengeance is not the best human emotion, but for a wraith, it is the ultimate punishment in fulfillment of a higher law.

The Story of a Vengeful Wraith

Thirty years ago, Texas fell victim to a series of strange deaths. They began during Dave's senior year of high school. There was a lot of the usual senior hazing going on by the senior boys to the underclassmen. The hazing could get bad at times, especially if the person was not part of the sports jock crowd. Dave was lucky enough to play on the football team so he was always exempt from the hazing rituals. He had seen what could be done and, looking back now, he wishes that he had the guts to stand up and stop it.

There was one kid in particular that was always getting picked on by a handful of football players. He was singled out because he was smarter and weaker than the others. The complete details are not known, but the morning after a football game, the boy was found at the bottom of a ravine dead. He had fallen from the high ravine and broken his neck. The ravine was a party spot for high school kids at the time. The event has investigated and labeled an accident. There were rumors being whispered in the high school halls that four of the top football players were involved with a hazing that accidentally led to the boy falling from the ravine. Dave knew that there was some truth to the story because all hazing stopped for the rest of the year and the four outgoing football players rumored to be involved were suddenly very quiet.

At the end of the school year, just before graduation, one of the four football players jumped from the same ravine and committed suicide. The boy was someone with a bright future. It was thought that maybe the pressure of knowing that he had caused another's death was too much. Or maybe he did not actually jump from the ravine. Maybe someone or something helped him go over the edge.

That summer, there was a strange rumor that since the alleged accident, the four football players had been plagued by a terrible nightmare of the hazing boy returning to kill them. The dreams were horrible and kept the four young men from getting much sleep.

A couple of years passed and Dave almost forgot about the deaths until he was contacted by a friend who told him that one of the three remaining football players had died in a car crash. He had driven off the road late one night and hit a tree killing himself instantly.

At the funeral, Dave saw a lot of high school friends that he had not seen in the past two years including the remaining two young men. They were powerful, smart, young men in high school, but now they looked beaten down by life after only two years. Both had dropped out of college and developed drinking problems. They looked aged well beyond that of normal twenty year olds. Dave wondered if what he had heard about the nightmares was true. The new rumor was that the ghost of the hazing victim was slowly killing the football players who caused his death. Dave thought this was a little bit crazy, but he could not deny the fact that the remaining two young men looked horrible.

Less than a year after the funeral, one of the remaining two young men put a shotgun in his mouth and took his own life. There was no suicide note found by the authorities. It was rumored that the family had found a suicide note that explained what had happened back in high school and the haunting visions that the four football players had lived with since the tragedy. The family supposedly destroyed the note and any evidence of the past to protect the honor of their son and family.

Only two years later, the last of the four young men died mysteriously in his sleep. He was found in his bed under the covers with his eyes and mouth wide open. His heart had just stopped beating. He did not have any known heart problems and his family did not have a history of heart disease. His sister told someone that it looked like he had been scared to death. Some people around town believe that the ghost of the boy who died in the hazing came back from the grave and caused the death of each of his murderers. Dave is still not sure what to believe about the whole thing. In the end, the town was left with a series of five deaths of promising young men all tied to one fateful night of tragedy.

the
Unavoidable Omen

The Unavoidable Omen

The unavoidable omen ghost is a ghost whose appearance signals that something terrible is about to happen such as a disaster, death or illness. These ghosts can be past family members or unknown specters. Omen ghosts can also be in the form of animals like phantom cats, hounds, and birds are the most common. The time frame between the ghost sighting and tragedy can vary from a couple hours to a few days. There is usually not any detailed information about the oncoming tragedy.

The odd part of these ghosts is that they manifest just before a tragedy, but with no specific information about the tragedy and without a way of stopping the tragedy. It is a compelling paradox; the omen ghost appears to warn the living about a tragic event that cannot be changed. Maybe the living are not supposed to know what the future brings, but, instead, are meant to be comforted by knowing that supernatural beings are watching over them. The reasons might be beyond human comprehension. Ghosts play by a different set of rules. Omen ghosts are in a different place and have a different perspective on life. Their supernatural perspective gives these ghosts an advantage. They know things about the future that the living is not allowed to know.

No one knows if omen ghosts are assigned to appear to the living or if they have to fight for the right to appear. Typically, omen ghosts will appear consistently to the same family line generation after generation. When the omen ghost appears, tragedy is always close behind. They are one of the most bizarre anomalies of the spirit world. The unavoidable omen ghost is a mystery locked inside a mystery.

Michelle had grown up hearing strange stories from members of her family. They talked about a ghost that appeared to family members just before someone in the family would die. The ghost was believed to be the ghost of her great-great-great grandfather. No one had any pictures of the man, but family members in the past had

recognized him and the word was passed down over the generations.

Michelle's grandmother had told her that she had seen the ghost only days before Michelle's grandfather had past away. The omen ghost appeared before Michelle's grandmother and stood there for about 10 to 15 seconds before vanishing. She could not remember too many details because it happened so fast and she was in complete shock. Two days after the sighting, Michelle's grandfather died of a sudden heart attack.

Michelle never knew what to think about the family ghost. She never told anyone about it out of fear that people would ridicule her. Despite her families passionate belief in the ghost, there were times that Michelle did not believe the stories until the ghost appeared to her.

Michelle awoke one morning like always and took a shower to get ready for work. She got dressed and started to put her jewelry on when a strange feeling overpowered her. She felt as if someone was watching her. As she walked into her bedroom, a cold chill came over her making goose bumps rise up on her arms. She did not notice anything at first, but as she turned to leave the room, she saw a man standing in front of her. The man was transparent. Michelle could see the bed, a dresser, and the pictures on the wall behind him. The apparition only lasted seconds.

Michelle realized, after the fact, that she had seen the family ghost, which meant that someone in her family was about to die. She called her grandmother to tell her what had happened. Michelle's grandmother had been ill for quite a while. She told Michelle that she thought it was her time to die. Michelle laughed and told her grandmother that she would outlive most of the family. Less than a week later, Michelle's grandmother passed away in her sleep. The loss was hard on Michelle, but the ghost gave her reassurance that there must be something more beyond this life. Michelle now wonders if the ghost will appear to someone in her family when it is her turn to die.

the
Ghastly Figure

The Ghastly Figure

The ghastly figure ghost is a ghost that appears disfigured and rotting. They look monstrous. They are not evil or violent, but they have a very disturbing and frightening appearance. With the exception of their appearance, the ghostly figure is a normal acting ghost. A normal ghost would appear visually much as they looked in life. If that person had a scar on their left cheek, then their ghost would have a scar on its left cheek. The ghastly figure ghost appears much like its corpse would probably look. These ghosts manifest with decayed and rotting skin. Their flesh is decomposing, their eyes are gone, their hair is falling out, and their clothing looks ragged and dirty. Their sightings are often accompanied with a rotten garbage stench.

Maybe these ghosts are aware that they are dead. Their perception is that they are dead and therefore they expect their bodies to be slowly rotting away. Their ghastly appearance is a direct result of how they currently perceive themselves after death. These ghosts tend not to use verbal communication. It is really unknown whether their visual appearance is intended to be a form of communication. Their manifestation could be a desperate plea for help or attention. The ghastly figure ghost seems to have an "all hope is lost" attitude. They feel that death is the end of all existence.

While being extremely frightening to living witnesses, these ghosts do not seem to be appearing for the sole purpose of scaring people with their image. Nor do they seem to have a malicious intent to cause harm to the living. Their appearance is gruesome, but that is really the extent of the damage that they conduct. These ghosts are alone and struggling internally with the reality of being dead. Until these ghosts can realize that death does not mean the eternal decay of the soul, they will be stuck on earth rotting away in their own mind.

The Story of a Ghastly Figure

There is a house haunted by a ghoulish woman on Martin Street in Detroit, Michigan. The house is named the Cole house after the previous owners Bill and Lillian Cole who were the first to experience the ghost. The modern house was perfect for the Cole family. During the early 1960's, Bill Cole would use the spare bedroom just off of the kitchen as a place to rest after his midnight shift at the local Cadillac assembly plant. The bedroom was small, but cozy and it was away from the rest of the daily noises in the house.

Bill went to sleep in the room one day and had a horrible nightmare. He dreamt that he opened up the closet door to find a blood soaked, disfigured corpse of a woman inside. He jerked himself out of the dream sweating and gasping for air. It was the most realistic dream that Bill had ever had before. It scared him enough to make him go to the master bedroom to sleep.

When Bill's mother stayed with the family, she slept in the spare bedroom. She complained that there were strange noises in her room keeping her awake. One of the noises was a pounding sound coming from inside the closet. She described the pounding as someone trying to get out of the closet. The family's pet dog would not enter the room so Bill decided that it was time to lock the door to the bedroom.

When a family friend came to stay, the Cole family was still in denial about the haunting. They let their friend sleep in the spare bedroom without telling him about the past experiences. A little after midnight, the man awoke from a deep sleep because someone was rolling him over in bed. He could see the back of a woman standing in his room looking out into the kitchen. She had long hair and was wearing a blue dress and fur coat. At first, the man thought that it was Lillian Cole. When he got up from the bed, all of the lights in the house went out. He walked into the kitchen and the lights came back on again. Lillian was in the kitchen, but she was not wearing a blue dress or a fur coat. The kitchen filled with a putrid smell that made them gag. Suddenly, the trap door in the utility room floor rose up by itself and then crashed back down. The police were called to the house that night. They searched the house from basement to attic without finding anything out of the ordinary.

To get to the bottom of these strange events, Bill decided to stay in the room. The activity began quickly. Bill had only turned off the bedroom's lights and gotten into bed when he began to hear rustling noises at the door. He thought that it was his wife so he yelled for her to go away before she frightened off the ghost. Bill's wife was not at the door and the ghost was not frightened away. The most hideous face Bill had ever seen appeared out of the darkness of the room staring directly at him. The eyes were empty and its' mouth looked like it was trying to speak, but a hissing noise was the only thing that Bill could hear. The ghost's body was like a rotting corpse. A foul smell emanated from the ghost.

Bill's plan had worked too well. He was not prepared for this experience. He jumped out of bed and bolted out of the room in utter panic. His wife and friend had to throw a blanket overtop of him and hold him down on the kitchen floor until he calmed down. While they were doing this, the trap door opened up again. The rotten stench of what smelled like decomposing flesh rolled out before the trap door slammed shut again.

Enough was enough. Bill and his family moved away from the haunted house on Martin Street. Many years have passed since that awful night. Looking back at the experience, Bill now wonders if the ghost was trying to show them something. Maybe there was a murder in the house and the ghost's real body was buried somewhere inside the house, maybe underneath the trap door. It is unknown whether the sightings of the decomposing lady are still occurring. The new owners will not answer questions about the ghost and do not want to be bothered.

the
Confused Victim

The Confused Victim

The confused victim is a ghost that has been created by a sudden and unexpected death. The unforeseen death left the ghost in a perpetually confused state with virtually no memory of their past life. They appear very pale looking with vacant stares on their faces. They seem distant and unattached. These ghosts make poor judgments and have almost no communication skills. They do not seem to be able to act properly or remember important details about the past.

The confused victim ghost behaves like a person who has suffered a head trauma. Death acts a lot like a severe bump on the head. These ghosts seem lost and confused. They are incapable of rational thoughts. They move slower than normal ghosts and seem to have difficulties concentrating. The problems of this type of ghost can be directly traced back to the unexpected event that created them. These ghosts have lost all control of their normal emotional processes. Other factors that contribute to their state of bewilderment may be denial and depression over their own sudden death.

There are clear indications that the confused victim ghost is not the same person emotionally. They do not act "normal." They have strangely remote personalities that do not fit descriptions given by people who knew them in life. Instead, these ghosts seem as if their consciousness has been altered by their sudden death. They are disoriented and unresponsive. For lack of better terminology, these ghosts seem like they are dead inside.

The confused victim ghost does not want to talk or intentionally communicate very much. When they do speak, they say things that seem bizarre and unusual. They will talk about things that do not make any sense. These ghosts are usually content to sit quietly and stare off into the distance with a blank glazed look on their face.

Frequently, these ghosts will erupt from their dazed condition and leap into a panicked state for short periods of time. For a few moments, they suddenly seem aware that they are lost and unable to communicate their thoughts and feelings to the living. They are frantically afraid by this lost feeling. They do not recognize familiar people or places and they do not respond to people who are trying to speak with them. At times, these ghosts can become easily frustrated and cry.

The problem with the confused victim ghost is obviously rooted deep in the psyche of the ghost's consciousness. Since ghosts do not have physical bodies, the confusion and trauma cannot be linked to a damaged brain or nervous system. In their state of confusion, these ghosts do not even have a memory of the event that turned them into a ghost. These ghosts do not have the insight to see and understand what has happened to them or the inner nature of life and death. Life and death are only a state of mind to them.

The Story of a Confused Victim

Susan lives in a house, which she and her husband bought almost ten years ago. The couple noticed right away that strange things were happening inside the house. Items were moving without explanation. Locked doors would be found unlocked and wide open. The couple would hear strange moaning sounds in the middle of the night. The couple joked that they had a ghost living in their house, but did not really believe it until they started seeing the apparition of a tall man.

The tall man always seemed to be as shocked as the living that would discover him. His apparition would fade away almost immediately after being seen. The couple would catch the confused ghost looking at things in the house as if it was studying the items. He was often found looking at the morning newspaper or at family pictures. Susan described the ghost's activities as be very much like that of a person with Alzheimer's disease, which her father had. The ghost had that far away lost gaze in its' eyes and never seemed to be aware of what was happening. There were a couple of occasions where the ghost seemed to be trying to mouth words and communicate just before disappearing.

The family learned from a neighbor that about twenty-five years before Susan and her husband moved in, there was a murder at their home. A man who was having an affair with a previous owner's wife murdered the owner in the back yard. This seemed to fit the ghost because there were several times that witnesses had seen the ghost standing inside the house staring out into the back yard, probably the location of the murder. When his attention was broken, the ghost would fade away. Susan also saw the ghost doing other odd things like getting up from a chair and walking straight into the wall.

Susan and her husband have stopped being afraid of the ghost. The couple has tried talking to the ghost and explaining who they are and why they live in the house, but the ghost does not respond to the attempts. The ghost has been seen dozens of times over the past ten years by Susan, her husband, and many outside witnesses who have visited the house. They are hoping that one day the ghost will realize what has happened and decide that it is time to move on.

the
Compassionate Presence

The Compassionate Presence

The compassionate presence ghost manifests to bring living people comfort and love. These ghosts are usually females or children. They had a sad life and are now seeking out people who are in similar situations to aid. They manifest to help the living in a legitimately kind and caring way. They are sympathetic to the pains of life and are willing to go out of their way to support the living and ease suffering. They are basically goodwill ghosts. They can be found guarding abused children or sitting in children's hospitals with them. They can be found keeping company with a lonely elderly person or with victims of tragic accidents. Anywhere there is misery in the world, these ghosts can be found helping people.

The presence of these ghosts is not seen or felt as a frightening experience, but strangely calming and reassuring. They seem, by all accounts, to be affectionate and gentle ghosts who want to do good deeds. They want to do everything possible to help ease pain and keep the living out of harm's way. They can attach themselves to a living person and follow them throughout their lifetime or just until they feel that the living person is safe on their own. They bring hope to the hopeless acting like a guardian angel.

These ghosts will do things like hold hands with the living, stroke the hair of someone who is drifting off to sleep, or just sit peacefully with the living. They seem to have a supernatural ability to tear down negative feelings. They want to use their own bad situation to bring peace to others. They want to make sure that something good will come from the bad experiences in their own life.

In many cases, other types of ghosts do not acknowledge the living. If they do, they are trying to express their feelings of suffering. The compassionate presence breaks the traditional ghost rules with its authentically friendly attitude. While the living can figure out that something tragic probably happened to this ghost in its lifetime, they are never made to feel or experience that pain. This ghost doesn't put any pressures on the living. It does not seek out recognition or acknowledgement.

Even with all the love and compassion that this ghost brings to the world, the compassionate presence is still just another lost ghost. Some people are never any good at taking their own advice. These ghosts are able to help ease everyone else's pain except their own. They are stuck in a limbo spirit world between life and death. It is a sacrifice that they have made to help others. The compassionate presence ghost puts forth an effort to lend a hand to the living and they do not ask for anything in return.

The Story of a Compassionate Presence

Brandon's grandmother was in critical condition in the hospital after having a series of several heart attacks. The family would visit on a daily basis in the morning and in the evening. His grandmother seemed to be getting better, but she had a long road of recovery ahead. Family started returning home from hospital visits telling stories of Brandon's grandmother asking if they had seen her mom.

Brandon's grandmother's mom had been deceased for decades. It seemed like she was just hallucinating from the pain medicine or as a result of her condition. She would say that her mom had visited and she could not believe how good she looked. She could never remember her looking that good. She would ask everyone who came in if they had seen her mother leaving. The family would play along and say no they had not seen her, but didn't try to explain that she was dead.

Weeks went by and the stories continued. Even the nurses commented that they could hear Brandon's grandmother talking to someone when she was alone in her room. When visitors would arrive, Brandon's grandmother always seemed to be doing better and she did not seem to be out of her head. She was calm and rational. She was aware that she was in the hospital and of what was going on around her, but she would continue to ask if anyone had seen her mother who always coincidently left just before visitors would arrive. She was still amazed at how good her mom looked. Brandon's grandmother told the family that her mother told her that it was not her time to die, but that she was going to stay with her until she got out of the hospital. Eventually, she did leave the hospital and lived for another year before passing away. It seems that the ghost of a mother would not let her daughter be alone in the hospital.

the
Invisible Watcher

The Invisible Watcher

The invisible watcher is an unseen specter that voyeuristically spies on the living. These ghosts sit quietly in rooms occupied by people so that they can study their daily activities. These ghosts create typical haunting activities (moving objects, making noises, apparitions, etc.), but seem most content to remain unseen. Common animals and house pets can sense the presence of ghosts and are good indicators of when an invisible specter is nearby. Pets will flee rooms quickly and growl, snarl or bark at seemingly nothing.

People usually know when there is another presence in the room. The living can "feel" when they are being watched. These feelings can be overpowering. The feelings of being watched by unseen beings are not always just a paranoid mistake. People can feel and react to the effects created on the surrounding environment by the presence of these invisible ghosts.

When ghosts are present, there are changes in air pressure. There are slight temperature changes. There are changes in the normal EMF fields and levels of static electricity. All of these changes are completely invisible to the human eye, but the skin and nervous systems of human beings can detect these small changes whether the people are consciously aware of it or not. These tiny environment changes trigger instinctual protection responses inside the human body making people feel as if they are being watched. These primordial responses are engrained into human brains to save people from becoming prey to a predator. People inside a haunted house often feel as if they are being watched even when no one else is around them. These feelings should not be ignored. In the cases of ghosts, these feelings are probably very accurate.

The invisible watcher ghost will observe, study, and learn every detail about the people who are the focus of their haunt. After the ghost learns enough about the person's daily routine, it can secretly participate in the routine. For example, if the ghost observes a person always reading a particular book in a particular chair at 8 pm, the ghost might try to participate by taking the book from the shelf and placing it opened on the chair prior to 8 pm. If the person is aware of the ghost, they will know what has happened and that the ghost is now somewhere in that room watching them read.

A very creepy aspect of an invisible watcher ghost is that they have a bad habit of frequently standing quietly inside a person's bedroom to watch them sleep or even sitting on the edge of the bed at night. People often wake up in the middle of the night feeling the ghost sitting on their bed. When they attempt to move, the ghost will rise up and flee the room realizing that it has been discovered.

Invisible watcher ghosts may be unable to willingly communicate directly with the living. They seem very content to watch silently. It is unknown exactly why these ghosts like to watch people and why they tend to shy away from normal ghostly communication. They do not seem to use any of the information gathered from their observation to purposely scare people. They do not have malicious intent and are not trying to make victims out of the people they are haunting.

The Story of the Invisible Watcher

Alison moved into her apartment less than one year ago. She noticed that small things were turning up missing and then reappearing in strange places, but figured that it was all part of the confusion of moving. Alison was in the process of getting a new job. It was a hectic time in her life. She did not have time to think too much about missing objects or why her dog would bark and growl in empty rooms.

Months went by and Alison was settling down into her new life. She was finally feeling content with the way her life was going.

She had more free time on her hands and more time to see that strange things were happening in her apartment. Her dog was constantly barking and growling and running from empty rooms. Alison started hearing unexplainable noises and footsteps in the middle of the night when no one else was in the apartment. Her dog would run into her room at night and jump into her bed scared stiff. Alison blamed her dog's actions on account of it not being use to the new apartment, but his actions still bothered Alison.

In the evenings, Alison would sit and watch her favorite television shows and read a series of books. Alison started to get the strong feeling that she was being watched in the room. The feeling would get more intense until her dog would start to nervously bark and growl. This process seemed to happen almost every night. Then, Alison started noticing that her books were being laid out on the chair. She could not remember putting the book on the chair and several times she remembers, without a doubt, putting the books away on the shelf only to find them back on the chair later.

One night, when her favorite television show was about to come on, Alison picked up the remote control and turned on the TV. Before she could push the channel button, the TV started changing channels all by itself until it stopped on the correct channel. This spooked Alison who finally started to think about ghosts. This type of activity continued until Alison could find a new apartment. She moved out after several months of living in fear. Both Alison and her dog now live in a new apartment on the other side of town. They are ghost free and happy.

the
Sad Denier

The Sad Denier

The sad denier ghost is a phantom that simply refuses to believe that they have died. They act as if nothing has changed and continue to reenact everyday events from their own life. They wear period clothing and might not acknowledge the presence of the living. Acknowledging the living would throw these ghosts out of character and make them think about their own circumstances. These ghosts have shut off the world around them to create a fake reality that resembles their own life.

Death is a shocking force. It becomes a trauma to the sad denier ghost. These ghosts are in a state of deep denial. In some ways, ghosts are not much different from the living. Both ghosts and the living seem to deal with death and grief in the same manner. There are stages of grief associated with death. Many times, the denial stage is the hardest to work through. Death is a very personal experience. The living will often shut off the world and refuse to acknowledge the death of a loved one. They go on with life as if nothing has happened constantly making excuses for why their loved one is not around. Death is a hard reminder of how fragile the human mind and emotional states can become. In time, there is an acceptance stage to the grief process when the griever can break down and let the stored up emotions out of their system. These ghosts are struggling in this system of grief. The sad denier ghost locks itself into a single moment in time that makes it feel as if it was still alive. That feeling gives the ghost comfort and support.

Death is something that will happen to every living creature. For some, death is such a powerful blow that they simply turn away from reality. The sad denier ghost continues to reenact aspects of their life in a continuous circle of never-ending madness. Each ghost will need to work through the denial and grief process on its' own terms before it can accept fate and move on. There is nothing that the living can do to help these souls.

The Story of a Sad Denier

The Hubbards live in a nice home in Georgia, which they share with a female ghost that refuses to believe that she is dead. The ghost can be caught doing normal household things like washing phantom dishes at the kitchen sink. When the ghost is discovered, she always appears to be in shock as if the Hubbards are invading her home.

The ghost has been seen rocking in a rocking chair knitting an old blanket. As soon as the ghost is seen, it fades away. The Hubbards do not feel threatened by the ghost. It has never done anything threatening to the family. Trying to find out more information about the ghost became somewhat of a hobby for the Hubbards. After doing some research, the family believes that the ghost was a previous owner who lived and died inside the house almost eight years before the Hubbards moved in.

Since the Hubbards felt they knew who the ghost was in life, they decided to try an experiment. Months later, the ghost was seen in an upstairs bedroom. After being seen, the ghost turned around and started to walk away. This is the point where the ghost usually faded away, but Mr. Hubbard spoke the ghost's name loudly and clearly for the ghost to hear. Instead of fading away, the ghost stopped and slowly turned around to face Mr. Hubbard. The ghost was transparent so it was not easy to tell, but it looked like the female ghost was crying. The ghost stood there for only a moment then started to fade away and vanished before his eyes.

It was over a year before the ghost was seen again. The Hubbards started to worry that they had chased off the ghost by speaking her name and may have forced her to remember that she was dead. When the ghost was finally seen again, she was doing the usual household chores and seemed surprised again by the presence of the Hubbards.

The Hubbards have decided not to speak the ghost's name or try to communicate with her anymore. They are not afraid of the ghost. She is welcome to stay in their house for as long as she wants.

the
Last Goodbye

The Last Goodbye

The last goodbye ghost is a spirit that appears to friends and loved ones just after its' death. They want to express a last goodbye to the people they cared the most about in life. They want to say goodbye and express feelings of love that they might not have been able to communicate while they were alive. Their appearance conveys hope and affection. They let the living know that they are not alone and that their suffering and grieving should be brief because they are in a better place.

The power of death is tremendously overwhelming. Losing a loved one can cause enduring emotional scars that never heal. Frequently, grieving people are left in a state of deep depression and endless mourning over the loss of a loved one. The last goodbye ghost returns one last time to express love and present a final farewell message to help the living cope with the pain of death and survive the grieving process. These ghosts want the living to understand that they are fine and that sometime in the future they will be together again. Their earthly pains are gone and they are in a place of happiness where they can watch over their loved ones.

The last goodbye ghost can also manifest to people one last time to fulfill a final promise. People make strange promises that they might never be able to keep even with the best of intentions. Death breaks all promises.

While technically a ghost, the last goodbye ghost will only appear one time to each person that it chooses. This ghost can appear to different people in different places. Their manifestation usually occurs a few days after death. Their expression of hope and encouragement allows the living to accept death and move on with their own lives. To the living, death may seem final. There are sometimes feelings that the living might never see the deceased again, but the last goodbye ghost shares a glimpse of the afterlife with the living to reassure them that death is not the end.

The Story of a Last Goodbye

Kelly Arnold's family got together to celebrate her birthday the night before her mother was hit and killed by a drunk driver. The family had spent the evening at Kelly's favorite restaurant. It was a good time. Kelly is grateful that they got to spend that time together before the horrible accident that changed everything.

Kelly was not ready for her mother to die, but who ever are ready to lose a parent? Her mother was robbed of life by a selfish act. Kelly felt as if a piece of her own life was taken away too. She struggled to come to grips with the loss. Loved ones, friends, and acquaintances were calling her to give their condolences. She was nice to everyone who called, but secretly she wanted to scream and be left alone.

Kelly spent the whole night before her mother's funeral crying into her pillow. She was awakened around 4am by a strange, cold feeling. She could smell her mother's distinctive perfume scent. It was a strong and familiar smell that was nearly overpowering. An odd light formed out of nowhere in the middle of the bedroom where it started to grow. The light grew larger and larger until it was the size of a doorframe.

Kelly's eyes focused on the light. She saw a person emerge from it like it was a door. Standing before Kelly was her mother's apparition glimmering in the light. Kelly immediately broke down and started to cry. She was happy and terrified at the same time. Her mother looked fantastic. Her hair, face, and smile looked perfect. It was a wonderful feeling to see her again. It was hard to explain, but Kelly said her mother seemed to be wearing a dress made out of light particles.

The apparition did not move or speak, but her appearance was like a long conversation. Kelly smiled back at her mother and wiped the tears away from her eyes. She was filled with joy. Her mother was fine and seemed to be in a happier place. The vision faded away slowly until she was gone and the room was dark again.

Kelly got out of bed and went on with her life. She does not know why she was blessed by the knowledge that her mother was okay, but she was happy to have seen her one last time and believes that they will both be together again in the afterlife.

the
Secret Life

The Secret Lie

The secret lie ghost is a ghost whose secrets from life have trapped them in the afterlife. These ghosts lived a lie and held dark secrets inside that eventually ate away at them creating a ghost. The lies and mistakes of the past made life a secret hell. Death arrived before the person had a chance to confess the lies or make amends for the past. These ghosts seek to find a way to clear their conscience. The secret lie ghost returns searching for forgiveness and understanding.

An example of this type of ghost might be a drunk driver who survived a car crash, but killed the passengers. No one ever knew that the driver had been drinking so he carried that secret with him until his own death. Another example might be a person who was playing with matches and ended up starting a fire that killed people. When they were asked if they knew anything about the cause of the fire, the person denied any involvement and lied about what they were doing at the time. These mistakes and lies eat away at a person's soul tormenting them and creating ghosts.

The secret lie ghost believes that if it can find a way to free itself from the chains of the past, it can pass on to another existence. Instead of moving on, these ghosts have become their own judge and jury. They know what they did was wrong. They never lived a day in their life that they did not regret their mistake. By taking responsibility for their own actions, they are trying to do the right thing, but it's too late. The time to make good and come clean for lies and other misdeeds of the past is before death.

Basically, all ghosts make the same mistake. They try to amend for earthly mistakes in the spiritual world, which doesn't work. The earthly mistakes end up controlling the ghost in the afterlife.

Worrying constantly about past lies and mistakes are heavy weights for any soul to bear. It's a constant circle of human blunders. The mistakes and subsequent lies messed up their life. Now, they are letting the same mistakes mess up their afterlife.

People often believe that ghosts are here to haunt the living, but the opposite is usually the case. Ghosts often end up haunting themselves. These ghosts do not need to seek out a way to reveal their mistakes and secret lies to the living. What this type of ghost has yet to learn is that in death, all secrets are revealed.

The Story of a Secret Lie

In San Jose, California, there is a mysterious mansion called the Winchester Mansion. The Victorian style mansion consists of one hundred and sixty rooms, ten thousand windows, two basements, forty-seven fireplaces, and forty staircases. Over twenty thousand gallons of paint were required to paint the entire mansion.

Construction on the mansion started in 1884 by the wealthy widow Sarah Winchester who was heir to the Winchester fortune. The Winchesters became extremely rich by inventing a rifle that loaded bullets with a lever mechanism. The Winchester Repeating Rifle was the gun of choice in the Old West. The easy to use weapon was responsible for thousands of deaths.

After the untimely deaths of Sarah's child and husband, a psychic told her that the Winchester family was cursed for all of the misery that their gun had caused over the years. Sarah was told to move toward the setting sun and start building a house.

Sarah picked up and moved to California where she started to build her mansion. The mansion was built from plans that Sarah would bring to the foreman every morning. They were drawn on paper or tablecloths. The bizarre design of the mansion was to keep control over the evil spirits and ghosts.

To the average person, the Winchester Mansion was a labyrinth of insanity. Staircases were built leading to nowhere. Doors would open up to long drop-offs in the yard. Tiny doorways were built too small for people to fit through. Cupboards were built with only a half an inch of space. Rooms were built around other rooms. There were secret passageways and trap doors hidden all over the mansion.

Sarah believed that the ghosts of bad men killed by the Winchester Repeating Rifle were still after her so she continued to build the house larger and larger. At one point, before a massive earthquake, the house stood seven stories high. The earthquake was so powerful that it twisted the room in which Sarah was sleeping trapping her inside. Since Sarah slept in a different room every night to throw off the ghosts, it took the servants several hours to find her.

The bell in the bell tower was rung every night precisely at midnight to summon the ghosts then again at 2 a.m. to signal for the ghosts to depart. Sarah really believed that there were numerous ghosts all throughout the house who wanted revenge against the Winchesters. Many visitors also believed that the mansion was haunted. Guests would hear strange footsteps, whispering, and the slamming of doors when no one else was around.

Sarah died inside the Winchester Mansion in 1922. Many people believe that her ghost now haunts the maze-like mansion. There have been many witnesses who claim to have seen Sarah's ghost wandering through the many rooms or seated at her favorite pipe organ in the parlor room.

The house is now open to public tours. Both visitors and employees have reported strange encounters with supernatural entities. In the end, many people believe that the mansion Sarah was built to control ghosts actually attracted the ghosts. It may be the family curse that actually trapped Sarah inside the mansion as a ghost.

the
Unfinished Life

The Unfinished Life

The unfinished life ghost is a common ghost of a person who died early in life. They feel that they have left unfinished business on earth. Like many other ghosts, they appear to still be trying to accomplish some of life's plans. They wish to return to life and finish their personal goals. These ghosts will continuously manifest with the hopes of finding a way to finish their lives. A murder, auto accident, fatal fall, drowning or an abrupt terminal illness typically creates these ghosts.

The motto of death is, "here today and gone tomorrow." No one knows the time of his or her own death. When death comes to claim its' victim, certain doors in a person's life are permanently closed. No matter what these ghosts do after death, they will never be able to bring a conclusion to their lost life. Sudden tragedies tear these ghosts away from their normal existence. The confusion can be tremendous and overwhelming. These ghosts are lost and confused, frustrated that their hopes and dreams for the future are gone. Most people live one day at a time never thinking about the day that will be their last on earth. Existing is all that living people know.

What journey lies beyond death's door is a well-kept secret. Human beings live out their lives always thinking of what lies ahead. People meticulously plan for every aspect of the future, but rarely calculate death into the plan. When death comes early, lives are left shattered and incomplete. Whether a person dies at twenty years old or eighty years old, there is almost always a feeling that there should have been more time.

The unfinished life ghost wants more time. Time to finish their life. They want a second chance to reclaim what they had in life. They want to accomplish what was left undone. These ghosts don't understand that their time on earth is over. Moving on seems like an easy thing to do, but when death smiles at someone, people rarely smile back.

The Story of an Unfinished Life

Jerry Segal inherited a haunted house in South Carolina. A ghost from the American Revolutionary War haunts the house. The ghost has been seen wearing his full military uniform. He can be heard walking around upstairs in his boots. Jerry says that he has

even heard whistling and what sounds like crying coming from one of the upstairs bedrooms, but no one is ever found inside the room.

Jerry does not believe that this home is the ghost's previous house, but the home of his fiancée. The rumor is that the soldier died in battle after promising to return to wed his longtime girlfriend. The two were pledge to have a promising life if it was not for the fate of the war. He swore he would return to her. He did, but after he had been shot and killed in battle.

Neighbors have come over and asked Jerry who the soldier was that they saw standing in the backyard garden. Jerry would tell them that it was the ghost who haunts his home. The neighbors did not believe him at first, but over the years, they have seen the soldier disappear or walk straight through the backyard fence.

The ghost seems to have a special affection for the garden. Jerry thinks that the garden is possibly the spot where the couple would meet in private. It also may have been where the soldier proposed marriage or where they said their final goodbyes.

The ghostly soldier is stuck trying to finish a lost life. He is yearning to fulfill the lost chance at love, marriage, children, and life. Jerry is not sure if the ghost will ever find peace, but he hopes that the ghost does eventually move on.

the
Instant Scar

The Instant Scar

An instant scar is an exact moment suspended in time where a sudden, violent, and unexpected tragedy creates a ghost. These events are usually extremely violent such as a murder scene or the location of a fatal car accident. The events are so terrible and traumatic that the tremendous human emotions involved explode outward from the event forever scaring the natural environment like a psychic atomic bomb. People who visit instant scar locations will experience apparitions, unexplained noises, screams, moans, and ghostly reenactments.

The haunting activity and its' ghosts will not, or cannot, leave the immediate area. Unsuspecting people who wonder into instant scar locations can inadvertently trigger phantom reenactments that can be brutal and traumatic to watch. The ghosts in these haunts do not always communicate directly with the living. Sometimes the reenactment of the tragedy is all that witnesses experience. Other times, ghosts can be seen inside the instant scar areas trying to communicate with the living. People can experience a wide range of paranormal activity at these locations. Many of these types of haunts only occur on the anniversary of the tragedy.

These ghosts probably went through life just like any normal person, never thinking about what tragedies might be waiting down the road. For any person, death could be years, months or minutes away. Some people believe sudden tragedies are a part of human destiny. They believe that tragedy is a set of unchangeable circumstances prewritten in the stars directing the future toward an unknowable purpose. On the other hand, there are also people who believe that all of the millions of tiny details in life that lead people to a tragic end are merely random and meaningless incidences. These ghosts see their fate as eternal torture. They are locked into a set of circumstances that they feel powerless against. Nothing can reverse the hands of time or undo the events of a tragedy. An instant scar is a single moment suspended in time that can never be reversed. It is a moment of fate that created a ghost.

The Story of an Instant Scar

Greg owns a house near a dangerous stretch of county road. Over the twenty plus years that Greg has lived near this road, he has documented over forty serious car accidents and at least a dozen fatal accidents. The road is a long straight stretch, but it has many small hills. Cars passing on the road do not always see oncoming traffic until it is too late.

Greg has become so accustom to the auto accidents that he has a video camera and several still cameras ready to document the accidents in the hope that the county will do something to help curb these terrible accidents.

A few years ago, Greg had a strange experience. Late one night, he heard the familiar sound of squealing tires followed by a loud crash. Greg ran outside expecting to see another hideous scene of twisted metal. Instead, there was nothing on the road and no sign of any cars or an accident. Greg looked around for a few minutes. Then he wrote the experience off and went back inside. A couple of nights later, the exact same thing happened. Greg heard the tire squeals and loud crash. Again, he ran outside to find nothing.

Greg thought that someone might be playing a trick on him until the night that he met the ghost head on. He was driving home late that night. He was getting close to home when he saw bright headlights in the distance. The headlights were coming down the road very fast when suddenly, the lights seemed to change lanes.

Greg braked hard even though the other car was still far away. He watched as the headlights swerved several times like the car was out of control. He heard the sound of squealing tires as the other driver slammed on his brakes followed by the sound of metal hitting metal. Greg could see the headlights go off the road, but he did not see another car or the collision. He hurried down the road, but when he got to the location, there were no cars or any sign of a crash.

Greg was still not sure exactly what was happening. He went home and looked over newspaper clippings of the accidents. He realized that a few of the major accidents had occurred in that exact area. At least two of the accidents had ended in death. For the first time, Greg started to believe that this phantom accident could be the ghost of one of the accident victims. When driving past the location, his car's compass will spin out of control. Balls of light have also been seen hovering over the location. Greg has heard the phantom accident numerous times and now believes that the location is haunted.

the
Lonely Lurker

The Lonely Lurker

Lonely lurker ghosts visit their final place of rest such as a graveyard, cemetery or unknown gravesite. The reason they loiter next to their own grave is unknown. They could possibly have a fascination or a special interest in seeing their own grave.

Cemeteries and old graveyards are the most popular locations to find a lurker ghost. They tend to haunt the areas around their gravesite. They can manifest at night with strange glowing lights or fast moving balls of light. They communicate with other visitors by gently touching them, laughing and giggling, playing practical jokes, and appearing and disappearing in front of people. The younger ghosts can be seen skipping between the rows of tombstones or playing other kid games inside the cemetery. Witnesses often report seeing people locked inside cemeteries at night, but after the authorities investigate, there is usually no one found inside.

Graveyard ghosts can appear to be happy or sad. Witnesses have reported seeing some these ghosts acting joyful and some sitting alone on a tombstone weeping. Maternal ghosts return to their children's gravesites. Frequently, the child itself is a ghost in that cemetery which the female ghost is searching for. The lonely lurker ghosts of children seldom seem to be aware of or understand what has happened to them.

Lonely lurker ghosts can also haunt old, abandoned mineshafts where they were buried alive. Mineshaft ghosts can be heard moaning and weeping from deep within old mine tunnels. Lurker ghosts can also haunt fields or backyards where they are secretly buried. Mysterious ghosts can be seen walking through flower gardens near, or standing quietly looking up at, the house in which their bodies where later discovered buried on the property.

These ghosts may return to haunt cemeteries and graveyards because their graves were desecrated or defiled. The violation of having their gravesite dishonored can be enough to stir up an irritated ghost. The ghost will protect their grave by scaring off any potential vandals and wrongdoers. If delinquents damage the gravesite or steal something from it, the vengeful ghost can follow the troublemakers home to harass them until retribution has been paid or the stolen item has been returned to its' rightful place.

In life, some people find graveyards to be places of peace and comfort. Graveyards can be quiet places to walk, relax, and think about life. Lonely lurker ghosts return to their graves to reminisce about the past, ponder the future, protect their remains, and find peace with death.

The Story of a Lonely Lurker

Bryan, from Iowa City, Iowa, had grown up hearing ghost stories about the local Oakland Cemetery where the ghost of Annie Oliver roams and an angel statue changes colors. Bryan was interested in ghost hunting so the local cemetery seemed like a great place to visit. He rounded up his friends and they went to the cemetery with some cameras and audio equipment. Their first trip to the cemetery was a bust. Nothing strange happened. After a few hours, the group went home, but they decided to come back the following night and try it again.

The group of friends went back to the cemetery the next evening. This time, they had different results. The group focused their ghost hunt on Annie Oliver's grave. Some of the members got a strange feeling as if they were being watched. The group began to have camera problems over the next couple of hours, but they still managed to take several rolls of pictures. They used the audio recorders to record voices of ghosts. At one point, the group recorded a female voice saying, “This is mine.” The group experimented with different ghost hunting methods until they had to leave the cemetery. Before leaving, one of the members picked up a small rock from Annie's gravesite. The rock could have been a piece of her tombstone. The group went home that night satisfied with their results and made more plans to return.

Later that night, the person who took the stone from the graveyard started to hear a voice in his bedroom. He could not make out what the voice was saying, but it was definitely a voice. When he got up to leave the room, he heard something hit the floor. He turned around to see that the stone he had taken from the graveyard had fallen off of his nightstand.

When he tried to open his bedroom door to leave the room, it was stuck - or being held closed by an unseen force. The door had never stuck before and there was not a lock on it. He pulled and tugged frantically at the door as the voices continued to ramble on, sounding like they were getting closer to him. Finally, the door popped open and the ghostly voices instantaneously stopped.

He stopped for a second and looked back into his room. The stone was back on top of his nightstand. He spent the rest of the night downstairs. The next morning, he woke up early and called Bryan to come pick up the stone. Together, the group returned the stone to exactly where it was taken from and apologized for taking it. Nothing else happened after they returned the stone.

The pictures that had been taken at the cemetery that night show strange light patterns and energy orbs. The group continues to ghost hunt in their area. Their experiences with the local ghost remain fresh in their minds. They now go into their investigations with more respect for the dead.

the
Spiritual Specter

The Spiritual Specter

Spiritual specters are the ghosts of priests, nuns, monks, shamans, and other types of religious and holy clerics. These ghosts will typically haunt holy locations such as churches, temples, cemeteries, and other places of religious worship where these ghosts frequented in life. Besides the fact that these ghosts were religious followers, they act exactly as other normal ghosts would act. There is no religious order in the world that does not have a spiritual specter haunting one of its' holy locations.

In somewhat of an ironic twist, many of the world's religions do not accept the existence of ghosts. Despite this disbelief, ghosts continue haunting. The spiritual ghosts do not care if people believe in them or not. Ghosts do not need people to believe in their existence in order to haunt. There is also a false perception by many religions that all ghosts are evil spirits out to destroy lives and their religions. The spiritual specters are, again, proof that the nature of ghosts is not inherently evil or destructive. Spiritual ghosts are uplifting and continue to provide help and compassion to people who need it most.

Old churches can be some of the most haunted buildings in the world. There are old churches in England with literally dozens of ghosts haunting the grounds. Witnesses report seeing strange glowing lights inside vacant churches at night and objects inside the church that levitate or move on their own. A spiritual ghost can light candles and watch over their respected worship shrines and other holy relics that may reside inside the safety of a church. Phantom nuns will continue to aid and comfort people that need help. Spiritual ghosts return to continue their spiritual fulfillment and to continue to give hope to the hopeless. These ghosts can also be on sacred missions that the living do not fully understand.

Spiritual specters may have also been mistreated, murdered or persecuted for their religious beliefs. In spite of their religious position, these specters could not escape the familiar ghost traps that other common ghosts fall into such as sudden death, an unfinished life, and the confused victim syndrome. These ghosts can be sad and upset over the circumstances of their death, but they always try to lend a hand to help out someone in need. Death is not the end. Spiritual specters do not let death stop them from continuing their holy work and from helping people.

The Story of a Spiritual Specter

Pengersick Castle has the reputation of being one of the most haunted buildings in England. In the forest located on the castle's grounds, archeologists found some very old structures that include an old chapel. Glass from the church's remains is now on display inside the Pengersick Castle. There is a story that an invading cavalier murdered a monk on the site.

The castle looks beautiful during the daytime, but visitors say that it becomes a very different and frightening place after sunset. Many visitors tell tales of a phantom monk that haunts the castle's grounds. The hooded monk can be seen walking through the gardens or inside the castle leaving behind the strong scent of fresh incense.

Nicholas was visiting the castle when he had his run-in with the phantom monk. He was bent down tying his shoe when he felt something quickly brush by him. He glanced up to see a robed man moving past him. The strong sent of incense filled the air. Nicholas thought it was strange to see a person there wearing a robe. He watched the man walk straight through a table and chair.

Nicholas stood up, his mouth hanging open in shock. The monk paused for a moment in the middle of the room and stood there. Then, he started to walk again, but this time, as he walked, he faded away into thin air.

Nicholas describes his experience as being like witnessing a car accident. Everything seemed to be happening in slow motion. The whole experience seemed surreal.

At the time, Nicholas did not know about the haunted history of the castle. He did not know where to go or who to talk to about his ghostly experience. He casually mentioned the phantom monk to a castle worker who, it turned out, knew about the monk. Then again, almost everyone associated with the castle knew about the phantom monk. The workers were full of stories about the mysterious monk.

Nicholas has been studying ghosts ever since his experience and continues to travel back to the castle every chance he gets. The monk continues to haunt the castle grounds, waiting on the next unsuspecting visitor.

the
Final Journey

The Final Journey

The final journey ghost is a ghost that appears as an unmanned vehicle traveling at high speeds over its' final route. The most common final journey ghosts are phantom cars, trucks, motorcycles, trains, and horse drawn carriages. These ghosts are a peculiar enigma because physical objects do not have souls. Therefore, vehicles should not have a ghost. Just because there isn't a visible apparition inside the vehicle, does not necessarily mean that there is not a ghost at the controls.

Phantom vehicles appear as real and solid objects. They emanate bright headlights and can sometimes be seen traveling several feet above the ground. Phantom vehicles seem very realistic to witnesses who believe them to be real until they suddenly vanish into thin air.

Phantom vehicles are always period vehicles; meaning that they are from a different time in history so they have a distinct appearance. There are sleek looking phantom sports cars from the 1950's and 60's, who crashed violently while speeding or drag racing, killing the driver and passengers. There are phantom black gangster cars from the 1930's and 40's, which speed recklessly down deserted back roads where gangsters used to dump their victims. In some southern parts of the USA, there are reports of phantom horse drawn carriages that bolt wildly down old dirt roads with and without phantom horses. There are even phantom steam engine locomotives that rocket through empty cornfields at the site of terrible train derailments where train tracks use to lay.

Phantom vehicles are more than just replays of a past event. They act and react to living people and other vehicles. Phantom vehicles have been known to speed directly into the path of oncoming traffic only to disappear right before impacting with another vehicle. They chase innocent pedestrians off of the road by steering straight at them. In some of these cases, the phantom vehicles are actually seen driving off of the road, crashing violently in front of shocked witnesses. The witnesses report hearing the tires squeal and the twisting sounds of metal impacting. They can see the fire and smell the smoke rolling from the accident scene. They believe that they have just witnessed an automobile accident until the phantom vehicle and the remains of the catastrophic crash disappear without explanation.

The exact reasons as to why these phantom vehicles continue to haunt their last route with this type of aggression are unknown. They appear to be reenacting the last moments of their life in the same way as other traditional ghosts. Veering toward innocent people and vehicles might be the only form of communication that these ghosts can offer. Maybe these ghosts are acting out of desperation and trying to do something different on that final route to change their awful fate.

The final journey ghost is most active on the anniversary of their crash or disaster. These hopeless ghosts are continuously traveling the same route while vigorously striving to reach an impossible destination.

The Story of a Final Journey

The strangest experience in Professor James' life happened to him while living in Provo, Utah. The professor was driving home late one night. The lowering train rails that keep vehicles away from the tracks when a train is coming stopped him. He sat there waiting patiently for the train to pass.

Down the railroad line, he could see a bright light in the distance. It was very dark that night, but the light was as bright as the sun. He heard the loud train whistle go off twice as it approached the crossing, but he could not hear anything else. He found that very odd because the trains that run on these tracks usually make quite a racket as they pass. Normally, the professor would have been able to hear the rumbling sound of the train's iron wheels rolling over the railroad tracks, but strangely, he could not hear any of those typical noises. It was eerily silent.

The Professor continued to wait on the train. He watched the light in the distance grow brighter and brighter as it moved closer. He rolled his car window down to listen, but there were still no sounds. The train was only about one hundred yards away now.

As he watched the single bright light move closer, he finally heard a noise. There was a strange clicking sound coming from the direction of the train. It was an abnormal sound that resembled metal banging into metal. Seconds passed. The train continued to barrel toward the crossing. The clicking noise changed into a terrible grinding sound. Professor James was starting to panic. He didn't know what was happening, but he knew those noises where definitely not normal. The train must be in trouble.

It was very close now, about twenty-five yards away and closing in quickly. The train's light was almost blinding. It hurt the professor's eyes to look directly at it, but he could not take his eyes off of it. He could not see a train behind the light. The noises were so horribly loud that the professor had to cup his hands over his ears to block out the screeching metal sounds.

The professor watched in complete horror as the light seemed to jump off of the track and start to skid straight for his car. Professor James thought that he was about to die. The light was sliding right at his car. He screamed out just before the train made contact with the side of his car.

Instead of demolishing his car and killing him instantly, the light seemed to pass right through the car and vanish on the other side. The horrible sounds of twisting and collapsing metal lasted a few more seconds then, they too faded away into nothing. The whole ordeal was over. Professor James was left sitting in his car in total shock as he watched the train crossing gates rise back up.

The professor was alone on the road. He was covered in sweat and nearly hyperventilating from the experience. He was in such a state of shock that he could barely drive. He does not remember most of the drive back to his home.

The professor spent the next week locked inside his house never leaving it, not even to buy groceries. Since the encounter with

the phantom locomotive, Professor James has scoured public records and old newspaper articles searching for evidence of a train derailment on those railroad tracks. He has yet to find the evidence that would help him understand his experience, but admits that documentation about past historic events is hard to find. Professor James considers himself a well-educated and rational thinking person. He did not believe in the existence of ghosts or the paranormal until one dark night when a phantom train drove though his car.

KEEP OUT!!
Diary
the
Elusive Mystery

The Elusive Mystery

The elusive mystery ghost returns to provide the living with hints and clues to a mystery in the hopes that the living will solve the mystery. Often, the mystery has something to do with the death of the ghost, such as an unsolved murder. The ghost hopes to expose the unknown murderer. Other times, this ghost is simply trying to reveal the location of a hidden object, such as a lost family heirloom. They divulge information that no living person could possibly be aware of to help solve a mystery.

As a way of providing hints, these ghosts will appear to the people that they wish to influence in specific places. They will move objects of importance so that they are found in a significant location or point to another object. The clues can be subtle or obvious depending on how much knowledge the ghost actually has about the key elements of the mystery and how much paranormal power the ghost can gather.

Not only does this type of paranormal communication have an important goal that affects the living, but it also lets the ghost continue to participate in life long after they have died. Ghosts want to be alive. They want to contribute in the daily routines and activities of normal life. Despite the fact that there might be a central purpose behind these ghost manifestations, this type of ghostly communication is just a way to allow the ghost to feel that it has purpose and meaning, even after death.

In a strange way, it is often believed that ghosts know everything. These ghosts can prove that idea is not always correct. Sometimes, these ghosts do not seem to know the final outcome of the mystery, like the name of the actual murderer, but they do have enough information to help lead people in the right direction. Even with all the clues provided by the ghosts, the living must be good detectives by deciphering the clues and gathering more information to uncover the truth.

When an elusive mystery ghost returns to provide clues about their own murder, the ghost can seem bitter and frustrated that their death remains unsolved. For whatever the paranormal reason, this ghost cannot haunt the murderer directly so they will do the next best thing- point murder investigators in the correct direction. The ghost will point out previously unknown bits of information that can be helpful in solving the mystery of their death. A rare few of these ghosts have the power to actually reenact the gruesome event in front of witnesses. Once the mystery is solved, the ghost is free to move on. Until then, the elusive mystery ghost will cut through the vale of death to help the living solve the difficult mystery.

The Story of an Elusive Mystery

Elva Zona Heaster was born in Greenbrier, West Virginia, in 1873. She lived with her mother, Mary Jane Robinson Heaster, for most of her young life. Zona, as she liked to be called, gave birth to an illegitimate child in 1895. About a year later, a man named Eramus Stribbling Trout, Edward as he was called, came to Greenbrier to work as a blacksmith. Zona and Edward met each other, fell in love, and quickly married.

A few months later, a boy that Edward had sent over to the house to see if Zona needed anything from the store found her dead inside her home. Zona's body was stretched across the floor with her feet together. One arm was at her side and the other was over her abdomen. The local doctor was immediately called to the scene, but he did not arrive for almost an hour.

By the time that the doctor arrived, Edward had already come home. He had carried his wife's body to an upstairs bedroom where he redressed her with a high collared dress. He had also placed a veil over Zona's face. The doctor examined her the best that he could with Edward at her side holding her head and weeping. When the doctor tried to do a more thorough examination, Edward became violently aggressive. The doctor was forced to stop his examination. He listed her cause of death as an "everlasting faint."

Zona's body was laid out in a wake. Many friends, family, and neighbors came to pay their respects to the family and say their final goodbyes to Zona, but Edward would not allow anyone to get close to the body. He had tied a large scarf around her neck and told everyone that it had been her favorite. He also placed a pillow on one side of Zona's head so that she could "rest easier."

Mary Jane, Zona's mother, went home and prayed that her daughter would come back form the dead and reveal the truth behind her death. Four weeks later, for four nights straight, Zona appeared to her mother at her bedside and told her that Edward murdered her. Zona's ghost expressed that Edward was abusive. He had attacked her and broken her neck.

Mary Jane took this information to the local prosecutor. There were already numerous rumors circulating that Edward had killed Zona. The prosecutor decided that it was time to find the truth so he had Zona's body exhumed and reexamined. The autopsy revealed the truth. Zona's neck had been broken. Her windpipe had been crushed, which caused her death. Edward was arrested for murder. The murder trial revealed more interesting information about Edward's shady past. Edward had been arrested several times for theft and he had been married twice before. Edward's second wife had died under mysterious circumstances. There were suspicions that Edward had murdered her too.

Mary Jane's ghost story had been ruled inadmissible by the judge. The defense attorney, in an attempt to show that Mary Jane was emotionally unstable and looking for someone to blame, made the mistake of bringing it up while questioning her. The door had been opened. The jury got to hear the full story of Zona's ghost appearing to her mother to point the finger at Edward as her murderer. The jury believed the ghost story and found Edward guilty. He was sentenced to life in prison. Before Edward reached the

Moundville state prison, a lynch mob captured and hung him. This case remains the only case in US judicial history where a ghost's testimony convicted a murderer.

the Malicious Ghosts

the Deceiver

The Deceiver

The deceiver ghost is a lying ghost. It uses false identities and gives out false information and signals. The lies and deceit are meant to control and manipulate the living. This ghost wants to keep people guessing while being constantly fearful. Its' lies help this ghost maintain an edge over the living, which is a very valuable aspect to controlling them. This type of ghost will have all the normal ghostly characteristics. The only thing that is significantly different from a normal ghost is the deceitful motives of this ghost.

The deceiver ghost should be viewed like a con artist. They will lie, trick, and steal at every chance. These ghosts cannot be trusted to any extent. The living should keep their distance from these types of ghosts. There is a chance that the deceiver ghost will become violent if it feels that it is losing control over its' victims. It sees violence as a way to regain power, but for the most part, this ghost is a coward. It will flee from any real confrontations.

The deceiver ghost will move and pose objects (such as dolls) so that the objects have a lifelike appearance. When the homeowners leave their house, the ghost will move and pose the object in a new position to give the appearance that the object is moving under its' own control. The deceiver ghost will try to get people to believe that it is the ghost of a lost child because people are more likely to try to communicate with the ghost of a child. Moving objects so that they seem alive and pretending to be a child are just some of the ways that a deceiver ghost seeks to manipulate innocent people.

The responses that these ghosts get from the living are very important to them. The more recognition that living people give these ghosts, the more power these ghosts will have over the environment. These ghosts thrive on fear and confusion. They will begin by testing their boundaries with small deception tactics. Then they will continuously increase the amount of deceit until it becomes obvious to the living that this ghost is only taking advantage of them. When the living ignores a deceiver ghost, the ghost will resort to poltergeist-like activity, such as throwing objects, banging loudly on the walls, and moving personal objects. Deceiver ghosts should be ignored and cut off from communication. Objects related to these ghosts should be removed from the house and destroyed. Eventually, as with all liars, the web of constant lies will eventually entangle the deceiver ghost and they will be exposed.

The Story of a Deceiver

Mark and Debbie Rice bought a collection of antique dolls from an estate auction. The dolls were almost one hundred years old and in very good condition. The Rice's were thinking of selling the dolls individually over the next couple of years and making a profit. Almost as soon as the Rice's got the dolls home, they noticed something bizarre about one of the dolls. It always seemed to be in a different location or posed in a different manner. The Rice's become aware of the obvious changes immediately and started to wonder what was happening. They would purposely pose the doll as an experiment and would return to find it posed differently. No one ever saw the doll move, but the doll was always in a different position from the last time it was seen.

The Rice's started to believe that their doll was possessed. The couple thought it would be fun to try to see if they could communicate with the ghost inside the doll. They invited some friends over to the house to hold a séance using an Ouija Board. The board said that the ghost possessing the doll was the doll's first owner, a twelve-year-old girl named Maria that had died from a fever. The girl only wanted love, affection, and a family. The Rice's considered that night to be a huge success and they started treating the doll like it was part of the family.

The more time that the couple spent with the doll named Maria, the more power and influence the doll seemed to have over Debbie Rice. Debbie was getting extremely attached to the doll. She felt that she needed to take it everywhere with her. Mark started to think that things were not right, especially with the doll. He wanted to store it away, but Debbie would not hear of it. She was happy with the doll. She carried it everywhere and talked to it like it was a little girl.

The situation was really starting to bother Mark who had a lot of suspicions about the doll. He could tell that the couple's relationship was suffering because of it. He also started having vivid nightmares that the doll was trying to kill him. He felt as if the doll was always looking at him in a weird way. He was trying not to be paranoid, but he really felt that something was wrong with the doll and that it might be plotting his eventual death when it had enough power.

Debbie allowed the doll to sit at the table while the couple ate and sit on the couch while they watched television. She was obsessed with the doll. Mark knew that it was time to end the doll's control.

One night, after Debbie had gone to bed, Mark went to the room where the doll was kept. He had already prepared a can of gasoline and matches and left them outside. When Mark tried to open the bedroom door to get the doll, the door only opened half way and then pulled back shut. Mark was stunned, but this proved his suspicions about the doll. It took all of Mark's strength on the second effort, but he was able to force the door open. The doll was starting directly at him. Mark hastily grabbed the doll and carried it outside to where he had hid the can of gasoline earlier. He found that the can of gas had been tipped over and most of the gasoline had spilled out, but there was still enough gas left to burn the doll.

Mark placed the doll down on the ground and poured the gasoline over it. He struck a match then lit the doll on fire. Mark swears that he could hear a loud growling sound coming from the burning doll. He watched it melt away then went back inside the

house.

The next morning, Mark was prepared to tell Debbie that he had burned up the doll. He expected her to fly off the handle at the news, but instead, she seemed strangely relieved that the doll was finally gone. The couple believes that the doll had some kind of hypnotic powers of control. They no longer believe that the ghost of a twelve-year-old girl named Maria possessed the doll, but that something terrible was in control of it. The Rice's are happy that the experience ended the way that it did. They know that it could have been much worse if the doll would have remained with them.

the
Nightmare

The Nightmare

The nightmare is a ghost with the ability to create horrible illusions meant to terrify the living into a state of control. They often create shocking visions of violent death scenes full of ghastly and unspeakable horrors. The visual scenes are brutal, dreadful, and extremely traumatic. These nightmarish visions are designed to drain the willpower out of the living victims. Every action that the nightmare ghost performs is a precise, well thought out plan intended for the sole purpose of creating misery.

The nightmarish visions can involve blood dripping from walls and ceiling. Victims will walk into blood soaked mass murder scenes. Shadowy fiends will chase terrified victims into rooms and then pound heavily on the locked doors trying to get inside. The nightmare ghost will create shocking scenes of dead bodies gutted and spread out across the floor or hanging from the ceiling. This ghost will find the fear of its victims and use that fear against them in awful visions. The visions themselves are not real, but they appear realistic and accurate.

The horrible scenes of gore and violence are meant to keep victims in constant terror. Fear guarantees that the living will not be able to think straight or make any rational decisions. In a vulnerable state, the victims of this ghost will make mistakes that they normally would not make with a clear mind. Continuous intense horror leads victims to sleeping disorders. The constant fear, lack of sleep, and pressures of everyday life put the victims into a deep pit of emotional trauma. The victims give into the fear and let the nightmare ghost manipulate every aspect of their life.

The nightmare ghost is different from the common horrific vision ghost in several ways. While the scenes can be brutal and disturbing, the horrific vision ghost shows real scenes from the past. The scenes are accurate depictions of terrible real life events. The nightmare ghost, however, creates ghastly visions of things that have never happened. It creates fake images of terror for the sole purpose of frightening the living into a state of complete control. The nightmare ghost will play mind games with its' victims. This ghost will cease attacks on its' victims for short periods of time, which is just long enough for the victims to let down their guard. When the victims believe that the ghost is finally gone, the nightmare ghost will begin to haunt again. The visual attacks relentlessly terrorize victims and drain the last ounce of sanity away from them. This ghost will not stop using nightmarish visions to terrify victims until they have completely ruined every aspect of their victim's life.

The Story of a Nightmare

The Brown family had lived in their picturesque Victorian home for over a decade before their haunting began. The home itself was over one hundred years old. It was a beautiful place and everything that the Brown family could have dreamed of in a home. Buying the home was one of their lifetime goals, but what they never could have imagined was that the home they cherished would eventually become a nightmare to live in.

The haunting began out of the blue and started small. The couple would catch a quick glimpse of something like a snake or black slug out of the corner of their eyes. The first visions were fast and timid, but the visions would advance and become much worse.

The Browns were tormented by a hideous vision of a grotesque massacre. They would walk into rooms to find a shocking, bloody scene. The scene was of a horrible axe murder where two children had been beheaded and dismembered. The room was soaked wet with thick, red blood. The scene would last a few moments until either vanishing or the witness would run away nauseated by the sight. The nightmarish scene was a little different each time. The children seemed to be posed differently for effect. The scene was always preceded by a toxic stench that would make people gag.

The nightmarish scene grew worse. The children's decapitated bodies were replaced with visions of the Brown children. The scene was imaginably gruesome and traumatic. The Brown family began to fear for their own safety and the lives of their children who had begun to see a horribly disfigured image in their rooms at night. The figure would loom over their beds and creep around in the room hissing at them from the darkness.

The Browns decided that it would be best to leave the home. They sold the property and moved away from the state. They do not know if the house is still haunted. The family does not know why they were singled out or what started the haunting. They believe that the entity that invaded their house was something evil, because nothing good could do what this creature did to them and their children.

the
Malicious Poltergiest

The Poltergeist

Poltergeists are difficult to understand since they aren't as simple to explain as a haunting. Poltergeists do not necessarily revolve around a ghost. The word poltergeist is a German word, which loosely translated means noisy spirit. A poltergeist is a form of malevolent psychokinetic energy, which builds up through different stages as the poltergeist progresses. Poltergeists can be emotionally terrifying and physically dangerous.

In early-recorded history, the Romans wrote about unseen spirits that threw dirt and rocks, smelled awful, and created loud unexplainable noises. These are all characteristics of a common poltergeist manifestation. The scientific debate of exactly what causes a poltergeist to manifest has raged on for decades. There are some paranormal investigators that believe poltergeists are connected to a ghost or some kind of evil spirit. However, most scientific studies advance the theory that points to an unknowing human agent as the culprit behind the supernatural manifestations of a poltergeist. The human agent has a psychic power called psychokinesis that allows them to move objects. The human agent is actually unknowingly controlling the supernatural activity.

Poltergeists advance in five stages. Each stage gives the poltergeist more energy, which allows it to develop more supernatural powers to influence the environment. The differences between a poltergeist and a ghost can be extremely difficult, if not impossible, to determine in the first three stages.

There is no way to escape a poltergeist. If the people involved in a poltergeist case try to run away, they will discover very quickly that the poltergeist will simply follow them. Unlike a haunting, the poltergeist energy will slowly build up over time while a ghost haunting will remain constant over time. At the end of the poltergeist's cycle, in the fifth stage, the poltergeist will almost always become violent and horrifying. The poltergeist will use all of its supernatural powers to inflict fear and bodily harm.

Each stage of a poltergeist will last a certain amount of time. The length of time will depend on each particular poltergeist. Each poltergeist will be slightly different from one another. The stages of a poltergeist might last days, months, or years. At the end of the poltergeist's fifth stage, the poltergeist will go dormant for a period of time then begin the cycle over again starting back at stage one. The stages of a poltergeist advance accumulatively. When a poltergeist reaches stage three, it will have all of the characteristics in stage three as well as stages one and two.

Note: Trent Brandon, the author of this book, developed this poltergeist stages chart. It may need to be updated or altered in the future when new poltergeist research information becomes available.

Stage 1: The Sense Attack

In the earliest stage of a poltergeist, everything will revolve around the basic human senses. Strange noises, abnormal smells, unexplained cold spots, and moving shadows are all very common effects of the first stage of a poltergeist. House pets tend to have a more acute sense for these types of activities. Pets will run out of rooms frightened or growl protectively at unseen forces. Individuals tend to have the unsettling feeling that they are being watched.

Stage 2: The Communication

Still in the early stages, the poltergeist's energy will advance and it will begin to communicate. Individuals will hear whispering, but won't be able to make out the words. People will hear laughing, giggling, and moans late at night with no explanation. Small objects, seemingly aimed directly at certain people, will fly across the room propelled by unseen forces. The cold spots have grown into cold breezes that whip through rooms. Static electricity will increase to an abnormally high amount. Odd marks begin to appear on the walls. Cloud-like apparitions also appear and disappear quickly. This supernatural activity is the poltergeist attempting to make its presence known. It wants attention and it wants people to respond to its presence.

Stage 3: The Electrical Control

This is the stage where a poltergeist begins to take control over electrical devices. They can turn lights on or off. They can short out electrical appliances. They can even take control over electrical appliances. The telephone will ring, but no one will be on the line or strange sounds and muffled voices are just barely audible. The static electricity is so bad that touching just about anything results in a painful spark.

The power of a poltergeist continues to advance. Unseen hands will touch, grab or push people. Writings appear on walls or household objects. Doors and windows open and close right in front of people. Unexplainable voices will shout out and scream loudly in the middle of the night. Shadowy apparitions appear randomly. Heavy objects slide effortlessly over the floor and large objects fly dangerously through the air.

At this stage, individuals fear for their safety. People realize that something supernatural is happening around them. The poltergeist utilizes the human fear as fuel to improve its powers over the next two stages. At this stage, most people mistakenly believe that they are dealing with a ghost. This is the stage that a classic haunting would fit, but poltergeists will continue to advance well beyond the normal powers of the average ghost haunt.

Stage 4: The Trickster Stage

This is the stage were the poltergeist's power quickly gains momentum literally becoming stronger by the day. The poltergeist begins to interact with the living by playing games on them. Hiding personal objects, holding doors closed, and turning off the lights in rooms may seem like the tricks of a playful ghost, but this is the way that a poltergeist learns what will frighten people. Furniture and beds violently shake. Scary voices shout out obscenities and orders. Unseen forces push people down stairs or grab and shake them violently. Vile smells fill the air. Spontaneous fires erupt in fireplaces and trashcans. Without reason, glass windows and mirrors shatter unexpectedly. People get nauseated and dizzy. The poltergeist uses this stage to gain knowledge of what people find frightening. It will use this valuable information in the next stage to create an atmosphere of absolute terror.

Stage 5: The Danger Level

This is the highest level of a poltergeist and its' most dangerous stage. Serious violence and life-threatening actions occur at this stage. People involved in poltergeist cases are terrified beyond the ability of rational thought. The poltergeist will bite, scratch, punch, pull hair, and aggressively attack people at random. Fires will break out while people are asleep. Electrical systems are used to create injury. Sharp objects fly through the air aimed directly to cause mortal harm. Heavy objects fall with the intensions of crushing people to death. Cases of human possession are rare, but can happen. Sexual assaults and rape are also rare occurrences of the poltergeist danger level. The poltergeist will do everything in its power to lash out at the living to create terror and carnage.

Anyone involved with a poltergeist should not wait to seek out professional help. It is vital that people realize that they cannot run away from a poltergeist and that there is no way to rationally deal with a poltergeist. Experienced parapsychologists should be brought in to deal with poltergeist cases. Victims may need to receive religious and psychological counseling, especially since there are almost always children involved.

The Story of a Poltergeist

Steve lives in a house in which two unrelated people have committed suicide. He was unaware of the homes history until after he moved into the house. At first, life in the house was normal. The family settled into their new home and the children, two teenage daughters, were enrolled at the local schools. The family liked the house and their new community. It seemed that they had made the right choice to move until some strange things started happening about six months after they arrived.

It all started with a car accident. The family was coming home from a night out when another car ran a red light and broad sided them. The crash was violent, but no one was hurt. When the family got home that night, they noticed right away that the lights were on inside the house. They were sure that they had turned off the lights before they left, but with all the confusion and shock of the car accident, they did not put too much thought into it. The doors of the house were still locked and everything else seemed fine.

Later that same night, after the family had gone to bed, they heard a loud boom coming from somewhere inside the house. Steve investigated, but could not find an explanation for the noise. A couple of nights passed and the family was awakened again in the middle of the night, this time by a series of loud banging noises that seemed to be coming from inside the walls of the house. The family also noticed that previously closed doors would be found open and lights would go off and on seemingly by themselves. Steve called in an electrician believing that something was going wrong with the house's electrical systems, but nothing out of the ordinary was found. As the week went by, the noises continued to get louder and more frequent.

One Saturday morning, while the family was just waking up, they experienced something that made them start to consider ghosts. They heard a crash from downstairs. The whole family rushed down to the kitchen and found all of the cupboard doors wide open. Everything from inside the cupboards was dumped out onto the floor. Dozens of pots, pans, and dishes were broken and scattered all over the floor. This was not something that could have happened by accident or something that could have been done by anyone in the seconds that it took the family to get downstairs.

Steve began to believe that his house was haunted. Furniture had been moving and the beds would occasionally shake. The girls started to hear strange voices in their rooms and their personal items would be mysteriously moved or turn up missing. Sometimes, the girls would return to their rooms to find that their stuffed animals had been stacked in the middle of the room.

The poltergeist was picking up momentum and getting stronger, but the family was not aware of what they were dealing with. One day, when Steve was walking through the family room, a videotape launched from its' shelf and flew directly at his head. He ducked to avoid it. The lights in the room started dimming then turned on and off. The paranormal events were slowly increasing throughout the house.

The family was now living in terror. The circumstances got worse when an unseen force started pushing members of the family and visitors. The oldest daughter was attacked and slapped numerous times over the following month. She seemed to be the main target for many of the physical attacks so she was sent to live across town with her grandparents. The attacks stopped for almost a week, but then the unseen force attacked the youngest daughter.

Steve scoured the Internet for information on haunted houses. He started checking into the background of his house. That's when he discovered that two different people had committed suicide inside the house. Steve also read up about poltergeists. He became certain that his family was dealing with a poltergeist entity. Both of his daughters were now staying at their grandparent's house, but the poltergeist had followed them. The girls were attacked several times at their grandparents and loud noises were coming from inside of the walls at that home too. Steve and his wife were also experiencing problems at their workplaces with electrical shocks, moving objects, and dimming lights.

The daughters moved back home and the experiences at their grandparent's house stopped. There was no way for this family to escape the horror of what was happening to them. Steve brought in several different people who claimed that they could get rid of ghosts, but nothing worked. The paranormal events continued to escalate until the situation was completely out of control. Dangerous fires were now breaking out in the home without explanation. The girls were having trouble at school because of what was happening in the home. They had started to see a therapist to help them cope with their troubles. Then, just when the family was at their ultimate breaking point, the poltergeist activity abruptly stopped.

Both of the teenage daughters later admitted that things were so bad in that home that they had considered committing suicide several times. Steve now wonders if the poltergeist experience pushed the other previous residents to commit suicide or if one of their ghosts was responsible for the terrible events that occurred. Steve and his family are very worried that the poltergeist will return. They have placed the house up for sale, but have yet to sell it. Steve makes a point of revealing the house's full history to any potential buyers.

the
Murderer

The Murderer

The murderer ghost is exactly what its name implies. It is the ghost of a murderer. In life, the person was a heartless killer and, in death, those feelings of bloodlust remain intact. These ghosts have no emotions and cannot be bargained with. The murderer ghost is searching to claim more human victims while continuing to live out their murderous bloodlust in the afterlife. These ghosts take joy in creating pain and suffering. They have a cruel passion to commit violent crimes. They intentionally terrify and attack innocent human beings and animals.

The murderer ghost is seeking to fulfill their need for immediate gratification through the taking of a life. They receive this sick gratification from causing fear, suffering, and finally death. They are sadistic monsters. They play mind games to terrify and torture their victims before attempting to kill them. These ghosts are without remorse, conscience or any sense of humanity. They are grim phantoms that are both menacing and vicious. They use supernatural violence against their victims. They attack with unseen hands to push, punch, strike, and strangle victims. They can savagely bite, claw, throw dangerous instruments or cause heavy objects to fall. They can take complete control of a home's electrical system and use it to cause physical harm, such as electrocutions. They will start damaging fires and can sexually assault victims.

Nobody knows what sparks the onset of psychotic behavior, but with these ghosts, this behavior is heightened with death. Many scientists believe that murderers have a mental illness or brain sickness that causes these people to commit senseless killings. It seems that a murderer's ghost is not set free from this unknown disorder after death. Death appears to make the passion for killing worse in these individuals. In life, these people may have committed some random violent actions and murders, but in death, they feel free to commit more random violence and senseless actions. The murderer ghost's main focus is to create misery and death.

Murderers are typically cowards. Murderers will never select a stronger or even an evenly matched target. A killer will always select a slower and weaker victim and this ghost is no different. These ghosts are basically cowards. They single out the easily frightened and the physically and emotionally weak to assault. They do not want a direct confrontation with a strong willed individual. They are powerless against people who stand up to them without fear. If such an overpowering individual confronts them, these ghosts will put their tails between their legs and flee.

Before attacks begin, these ghosts will typically leave symbols, which can be seen as warning signs. Common warning signs are strange marks and symbols appearing on walls or other physical structures. Before the violence escalates to life threatening levels, the murderer ghost will test its, boundaries by holding down their victims in bed or gently nudging them down steep stairs. Any violent or threatening warning signs should be taken seriously and not ignored or neglected.

The murderer ghost has all the same violent and threatening characteristics as a poltergeist, but like other ghosts, they are locked into one area and cannot leave that location. These ghosts can usually be traced back to a real life murderer. The location that the ghost haunts is usually the location of their death or the location of one of their most violent murders, typically a mass murder scene. While they are powerful, their supernatural influence is limited and each murder ghost will be different from another.

The murderer ghost is a predator. They hunt the weak and helpless. They are always searching for that one person or family that fits their requirements. They are invisible monsters that needlessly slaughter life. They should be considered extremely dangerous and taken very seriously. The murderer ghost is the darkest edge of mankind. It's a supernatural psychopath.

When the Leals moved into their new house, it was a dream come true. It was their first home and they were very excited. However, from day one, the Leals noticed that strange things were happening. The family dog did not want to be inside the house. When it was forced to be inside, it would whine and whimper to be let out. The dog was a pampered pet. He did not like to be outdoors before they had moved into the new house. The Leals noticed that a stain on the upstairs carpet seemed to be getting larger and darker by the week. The stain could be cleaned up, but it would begin to reform on the carpet. The couple started hearing blood curdling screams from what sounded like a female's voice. The screams would awaken the couple in the middle of the night. There was never an explanation. Soon after, the screams were joined with a very loud banging noise. The noise sounded like gunshots. The Leals were terrified then, but things were about to get must worse.

The furniture started to shake uncontrollably. An unseen force started pushing people down steps or toward the burners on the kitchen stove. Mr. Leal became worried for their safety and started asking around about the history of the house. He discovered, from one of the neighbors, that back in the early 1970's, a man brutally murdered his wife by shooting her with a shotgun in the upstairs room that now has the strange growing stain on the carpet. Mr. Leal also learned that the carpet was not the original. It had been replaced several times by other owners and the stain always reappears on the new carpet.

Mr. Leal had a local minister bless the home, which seemed to be a mistake. The night of the blessing, the Leals were terrified by a series of attacks that involved pushing, slapping, and biting by unseen forces. Mr. Leal did not realize that the blessing was a mistake and searched out the help of a local psychic to come into the house. The psychic claimed that the ghosts of the murdered woman and her murderer husband were still present inside the house. The psychic felt the presence of evil. The evil entity wanted to kill the Leals. The psychic made a plea for help to the ghost of the murdered woman.

The psychic claimed that the woman was stuck in a ghostly reenactment of the murder, but the ghostly woman was either unwilling or unable to help the Leal family. The haunting continued despite the plea for help to the female ghost.

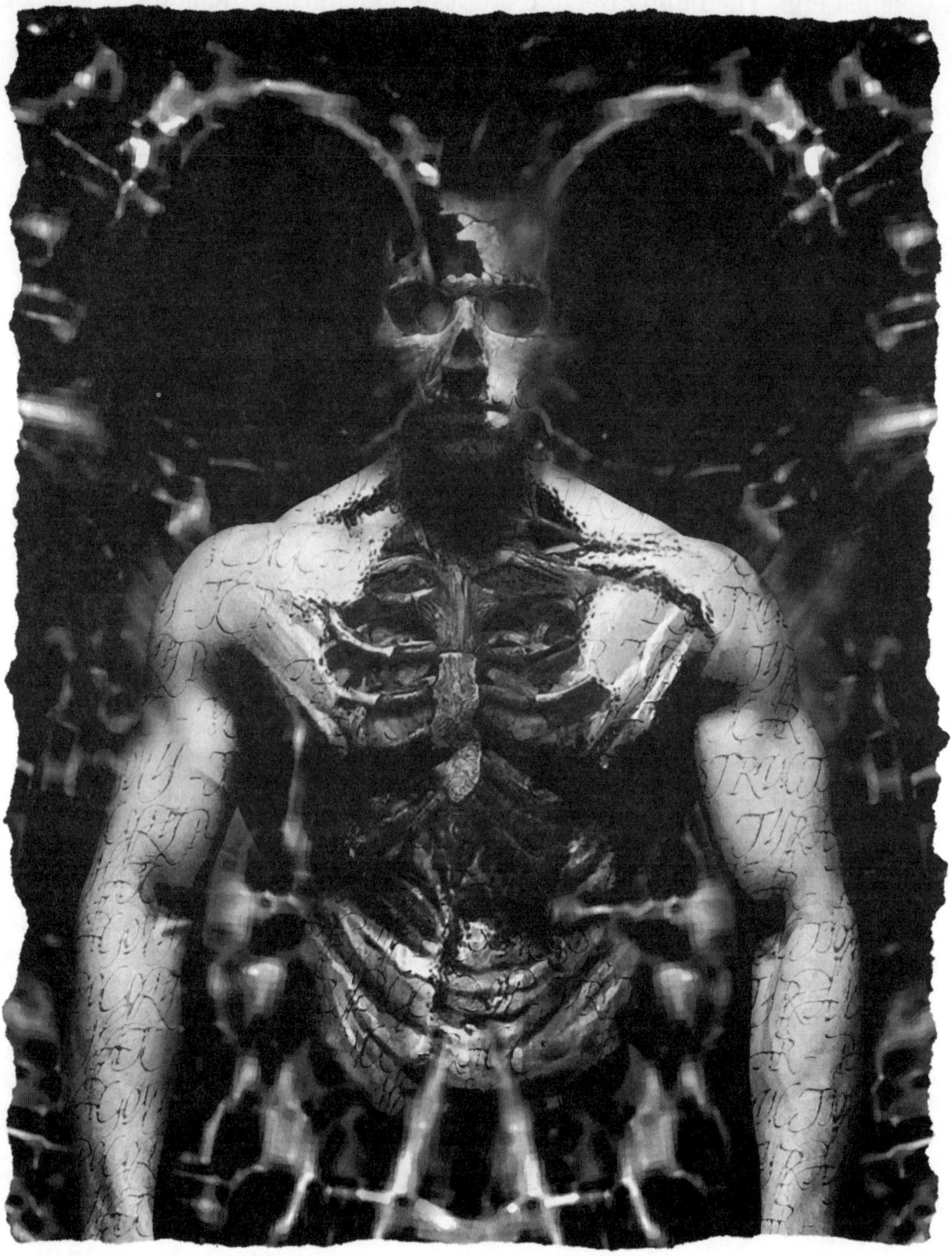

The Leals noticed strange burn marks on the walls, carpets, and in a trashcan. The Leals were at a loss to find a cause for the mysterious burn marks until one evening while they were watching television. The television screen started to flicker and flash and then, without warning, a small piece of the living room wall burst into flames. Mr. Leal jumped to his feet and patted the fire out. Later that same night, when Mrs. Leal was in the shower, she began screaming. Mr. Leal ran to his wife's aid in the bathroom. When she was getting into the shower, she saw a dark shadow glide across the bathroom. She heard something at the bathroom counter. Suddenly, the hair dryer was thrown overtop of the shower curtain and into the shower with her. The hair dryer was unplugged when she got into the shower, but it was plugged in when it was thrown over the curtain rod. Luckily, the cord was not long enough to let the hair dryer hit the water.

After this attack, the Leals packed up some clothing and personal items. They left the house to go stay with relatives. The Leals have since sold the house and moved on with their lives. They do not know if the stain is still appearing on the upstairs carpet or if the ghost of the murderer is terrorizing the new homeowners.

the
Destroyer

The Destroyer

The destroyer ghost is often referred to as, "the false ghost," simply because most paranormal researchers do not believe there are enough facts to support that these beings are ghosts. Its' supernatural powers are far beyond any normal ghost. The destroyer does not really fit in with the other evil spirits (Deceiver, Nightmare, Poltergeist, and Murderer) in this category. They have characteristics that no other ghost seems capable of controlling. They are foul, cunningly ruthless, and basically unstoppable creatures. They terrorize victims with the final intentions of possession and execution. They have an utter contempt for mankind and all life in general. They want nothing more than to create absolute chaos, death, and devastation. They are extremely violent and extraordinarily powerful.

These beasts are accompanied with vile smells, deep and loud pounding sounds, bellowing shrieks, and howling noises. The destroyer will viciously attack and, if it gets the chance, brutally murder anyone who gets in the way. It will sexually assault and rape men, woman, and children. Destroyers are capable of shaking the foundations of a house until the walls and ceilings crack and the windows shatter. They attract hordes of filthy insects and create sickness and disease. They will burn homes to the ground with fierce fires. Destroyers will cause people to act out of character to do and say terrible things that they would have never done normally. They are the harbingers of disaster and ill fortune.

The destroyer is a black plague. They sweep into an area without warning bringing sickness and grief. Destroyers surround everything in a dark cloud of destruction. They ruin lives and command great amounts of absolute madness. Once the destroyer has invaded a location, it will act like a ferocious parasite draining all of the energy and life from the location and from the living. They will randomly and sadistically assault men, woman, children, and pets. The destroyer seeks to eventually possess a living host who they can control and manipulate. Their mission is only complete when they have succeeded in massacring all who have ventured into their path of total annihilation. The destroyer is the awful stuff of nightmares. It does not have any redeemable qualities. Simply put, the destroyer is the worst of the worst.

Unlike a poltergeist, there are no levels or stages. It is always in high gear and it is always creating havoc. The destroyer ghost seems to be nomadic. They can drift from location to location at anytime. They can manifest in one location for a short period of time only to leave without reason and appear in a nearby location. The destroyer does not need to attach itself to a specific location or person. They cannot be traced back to a previously living person. Destroyers have their own unknown horrifying agenda. They are uncontrollable and will continuously do things that are depraved, brutal, and disgusting. The best advice that can be given to someone who is confronted by a destroyer ghost is to quickly run away.

The Story of a Destroyer

The Roberts' had lived in the same house for nearly eighteen years. They had never experienced ghosts or any other paranormal activity in all of their years at the residence. The family loved their home and had no intentions of leaving it until their lives were turned upside down by an unknown entity that wanted to destroy them.

Mr. and Mrs. Roberts were unaware that two of their three young children had begun to dabble with strange magic rituals and use an Ouija Board. It was not long afterwards, that strange things began happening in the Roberts' home. An odd smell filled the house. The smell was a mild, rotting stench. It filled different areas of the house. No matter what was done, nothing could get rid of it. Soon afterwards, the family started hearing strange voices when nobody else was around. The children were also hearing whispering voices and seeing shadows move in their rooms at night. A loud, deep pounding echoed out of the basement and attic.

The family was afraid to be inside their own house. The strange voices increased to shouts. Odd black marks began to form on the walls in all of the rooms. Insects seemed to be flooding into the house. The house smelled terrible and the bugs were swarming. A shadowy figure loomed inside the house. Members of the family would see shadows pass through walls followed by the stench. Food in the refrigerator would spoil after a couple of hours. Doors started to slam shut as people walked toward them.

One of the young boys started feeling sick all of the time. He developed severe stomach cramps, a fever, and nausea. The family did what they could for him. Doctors prescribed antibiotics, but nothing seemed to help. The boy's condition worsened.

The last straw occurred when Mr. Roberts went out to the garage to retrieve a pair of work gloves. A large box mysteriously fell from a shelf landing directly on Mr. Roberts' head knocking him unconscious. He awakened while his frantic wife was desperately pulling him from the garage. He was coughing and gagging and felt very woozy. There was an awful smell inside the garage, but it was not the normal stench. It smelled like car exhaust.

Mrs. Roberts had just returned from the store to find Mr. Roberts unconscious in the garage. The car in the garage was running and the keys were locked inside. The garage door was also not working so she could not get the door to open up. Mr. Roberts made it out of the garage, but he probably would have died with only a few minutes more of exposure to the toxic exhaust fumes. At this point, the family realized they had a serious problem.

The Roberts' young boy's health continued to get worse. He had started to talk in a strange tone and, seemingly, in a different language. He would mumble unrecognizable sentences and yell angrily at people who got too close to him. The boy seemed to be developing a second personality.

About this same time, the trees in the yard developed a fungus that killed all of them. The bushes and the grass seemed to be brown and frail despite the nice weather. Even though the house was painted only four years prior, the paint started to peel and split. It was as if the yard and house were becoming ill and dying.

The family's local priest was brought to the home. The sick boy immediately attacked him scratching his face badly and almost seriously damaging one of his eyes. The small boy had to be forcefully pulled from the priest by three grown adults. Later, the boy was diagnosed as being possessed. He was taken away to an undisclosed location for an exorcism.

The house was deemed unsalvageable so the family placed it up for sale. It was only then that the family learned that their children had been performing black magic rituals in the basement of their home. Dozens of ritual and summoning books were found. The oldest boy finally confessed to using the books and the Ouija Board with his brother to summon ghosts.

The family moved away from their once beautiful home. The Roberts' son was returned to them normal and healthy after only a couple of weeks. The family never asked the boy about the exorcism. The family's new house seems to be spirit free. They are very grateful for the help that they received from many different people during this terrible time. The terror has ended for this family, but they will never forget the damage that this experience created.

The End...

From the Author:

I want to thank all of the wonderful people who emailed their ghost stories and shared their experiences. I am extremely grateful that I have gotten to know so many good people while ghost hunting. I wish luck, knowledge and safety to all of the ghost hunters and to the people currently living with a ghost.

Sincerely,
Trent Brandon

References

Alcock, E. James. *Parapsychology: Science or Magic? A Psychological Perspective.* Oxford: Pergamon, 1981.

Auerbach, Loyd. *ESP, Hauntings and Poltergeists: A Parapsychologist's Handbook.* New York: Warner Books, 1986.

Bayless, Raymond. *The Enigma of the Poltergeist.* West Nyack, NY: Parker Publishing Co., 1967.

Cohen, Daniel. *The Encyclopedia of Ghosts.* New York: Dodd, Mead & Co., 1984.

Deitz, Dennis. *The Greenbrier Ghost and Other Strange Stories.* West Virginia: Mountain Memories Books, 1990.

Dickinson, Rachel. Summers, Lori. *The Ghost Hunter's Handbook.* Price Stern Sloan Pub, 2002.

Father Leo Schmid. *Wen Die Toten Reden (When the Dead Speak).* Vatican: 1976

Gross, Michael. *The Evidence for Phantom Hitchhikers.* Wellingborough, Northamptonshire, England: The Aquarian Press, 1984.

Guiley, Rosemary Ellen. *Harper's Encyclopedia of Mystical & Paranormal Experience.* Edison, New Jersey: Castle Books, 1991.

Guiley, Rosemary Ellen. *The Encyclopedia of Ghosts and Spirits.* New York: Facts on File, 1992.

Haining, Peter. *A Dictionary of Ghosts.* London, 1982.

Harkleroad, Tim. *The Complete Haunted House Book.* Bristol, TN: Moonlighting Publications, 1998.

Hauch, Dennis William. *Haunted Places: The National Directory.* New York: Penguin Books, 1996.

Holzer, Hans. *America's Haunted Houses*. Stanford, CT: Longmeadow Press, 1991.

Hope, Val. *The Paranormal Investigator's Handbook.* Collins & Brown, 1999.

Kaczmarek, Dale. *Field Guide to Spirit Photography.* Alton, Illinois: Whitechapel Press & the American Ghost Society, 2002.

MacKenzie, Andrew. *Hauntings and Apparitions.* London: Heinemann Ltd., 1982.

May, Antoinette. *Haunted Houses of California: A Ghostly Guide to Haunted Houses and Wandering Spirits.* Wide World Pub Tetra, 1993.

Oester, Dave. Gill, Sharon. *The Haunted Reality.* Starwest Images, 1996.

Osborne-Thomason, Natalie. *The Ghost-Hunting Casebook.* London: Blandford Press, 1999.

Rule, Ann. Rule, Leslie. *Coast to Coast Ghosts: True Stories of Hauntings Across America.* Kansas City, MO: Andrews McMeel Publishing, 2001.

Sellier E. Charles, and Meier, Joe. *The Paranormal Sourcebook : A Complete Guide to All Things Otherworldly.* Lowell House, 1999

Taylor, Troy. *The Ghost Hunter's Guidebook.* Alton, Illinois: Whitechapel Press & the American Ghost Society, 2000.

Time Life Books. *Mysteries of the Unknown: Phantom Encounters.* Alexandria, Virginia: Time Life Books, 1988.

Underwood, Peter. *Ghosts and How to See Them.* Osnaburgh Street, London: Anaya Publishers Limited, 1993.

Underwood, Peter. *Peter Underwood's Guide to Ghosts and Haunted Places.* England: Piatkus Books, 2000.

Wilson, Colin. *Poltergeist; A Study in Destructive Haunting.* St. Paul, Minnesota: Llewellyn Publications, 1993.

Wookyard, Chris. *Ghost Hunter's Guide to Haunted Ohio*. Dayton, OH: Kestrel Publication, 2000.

The Gauss Master

This **EMF** (**E**lectro-**M**agnetic **F**ield) **Detector** is the most widely utilized meter for ghost hunter's and paranormal investigators.

This devices can pick up electronic and magnetic fields over different frequencies. It's a theory that when ghosts are present they disrupt the electromagnetic fields. This EMF detector will detect these disruptions.

Hand-held, lightweight and durable, with two easy to read scales (0-1 mG, & 0-10 mG), and dramatic audio signal. The favorite meter for demonstrating the presence of EMFs fields. *Requires one 9V battery (Included).*

As a guideline each person in your ghost-hunting group should have at least one EMF detector on hand.

Gauss Master Price = $49.00

- Shipping to US add $4.00
- Shipping to Canada add $6.00
- Other international orders must visit our website to place an order.

- If you are ordering more than one item from this book add $1.50 for each additional item to the shipping change listed above.

Make all payments to **Zerotime Publishing, 10721 Green Lawn St. Minerva, Ohio 44657.** Payments can be made with a Cashiers Check, a Personal Check, or a Money Order for the total amount of $49.00 plus shipping. *All prices are in US Dollars.* Only payments made out to US Dollars will be accepted.

Visit us online at http://www.zerotime.com/storefront/
Email: trent@zerotime.com

Note: Along with your payment please include the Item Name (Gauss Master EMF), Your Return Address, Telephone Number, and Your Email address (if you have one). Clearly Written!

Infrared Thermometer

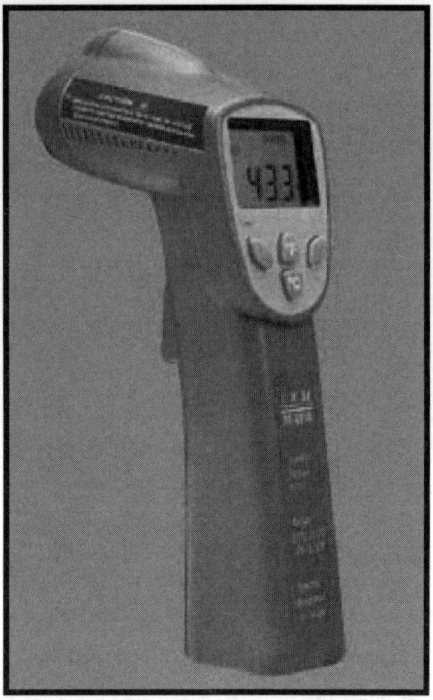

The Remote **IR Thermometer** is an amazing piece of ghost hunting equipment.

This pistol-grip meter (with laser pointer for pinpoint accuracy) will measure temperatures from 0° all the way up to 600°F at a safe distance. Offers an amazing 2% accuracy and a resolution of 1°F. Field of view is 6:1, emissivity fixed at 0.95.

F/C changable readout. Backlit LCD readout is easy to see, even in dim lighting.

Ghost Hunter's can use this device to detect and pin-point both abnormal "cold spots" and "hot spots" common with ghosts and paranormal activity. The next time you feel a cold chill run over your body you will know exactly how cold it was and which direction it traveled. (9 volt battery included)

Pistol Grip. 6 inches tall, 1.50 inches wide. All products guaranteed to work!

IR Thermometer Price = $99.00

- Shipping to US add $4.00
- Shipping to Canada add $6.00
- Other international orders must visit our website to place an order.

- If you are ordering more than one item from this book add $1.50 for each additional item to the shipping change listed above.

Make all payments to **Zerotime Publishing, 10721 Green Lawn St. Minerva, Ohio 44657.** Payments can be made with a Cashiers Check, a Personal Check, or a Money Order for the total amount of $99.00 plus shipping. *All prices are in US Dollars.* Only payments made out to US Dollars will be accepted.

Visit us online at http://www.zerotime.com/storefront/
Email: trent@zerotime.com

Note: Along with your payment please include the Item Name (IR Thermometer), your Return Address, Telephone Number, and your Email address (if you have one). Clearly Written!

Natural EM Meter

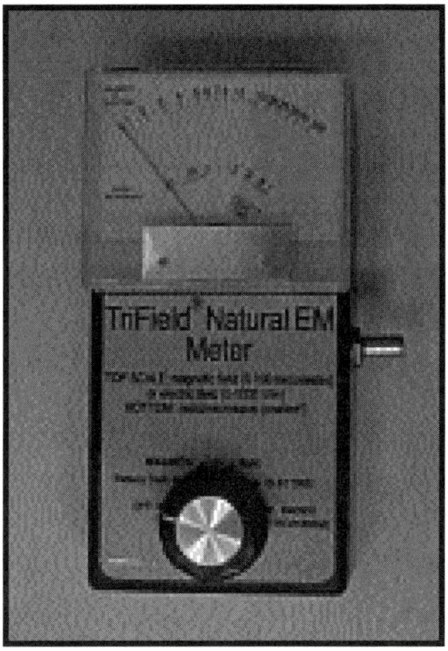

The Natural EMF Meter detects microwaves and changes in extremely weak static electric and magnetic fields. Using both a needle type meter and audible tone, it detects: distant radio transmitters, geomagnetic storms, unusual magnetic solar activity, electrical activity of thunderstorms, and concealed surveillance bugs.

This EMF Meter is used by professional paranormal investigators. It can detect even the slighest change in the electro-magnetic fields.

Detects the electrical presence of a person. Sensitive to changes in electric fields of as little as 3 V/m with a full scale deflection at 1000 V/m. Will measure magnetic field changes as small as 0.5% of the Earth's magnetic field (2.5 mG) and as high as 100 microtesla (1000 mG). 9v battery included. One year manufacturer's warrantee. Handheld. 5 inches tall, 2.50 inches wide, 2 inches thick. Black Color. All products guaranteed to work!

Natural EM Meter Price = $180.00

- Shipping to US add $4.00
- Shipping to Canada add $6.00
- Other international orders must visit our website to place an order.

- If you are ordering more than one item from this book add $1.50 for each additional item to the shipping change listed above.

Make all payments to **Zerotime Publishing, 10721 Green Lawn St. Minerva, Ohio 44657.** Payments can be made with a Cashiers Check, a Personal Check, or a Money Order for the total amount of $180.00 plus shipping. *All prices are in US Dollars.* Only payments made out in US Dollars will be accepted.

Visit us online at http://www.zerotime.com/storefront/
Email: trent@zerotime.com

Note: Along with your payment please include the Item Name (Natural EM Meter), your Return Address, Telephone Number, and your Email address (if you have one). Clearly Written!